THE INDIANA FLAG

Who Really Designed It?

DAVID B. REDDICK

ISBN: 978-1-955622-04-2 (hardcover)
978-1-955622-03-5 (paperback)

Published by

Fideli Publishing, Inc.
119 W. Morgan St.
Martinsville, IN 46151
www.FideliPublishing.com

To my lovely wife, Rebecca,
and to
Janice Bolinger, my early collaborator

TABLE OF CONTENTS

INTRODUCTION

M y interest in this project first began in 2017 when I asked myself this question: What information, if any, existed about the Indiana state flag prior to 1917?

My curiosity had been aroused the year before after the Indiana Historical Bureau erected a marker in downtown Mooresville to mark the 100th anniversary of the state flag designed by local resident Paul Hadley. The wording on the marker focused primarily on the flag after 1917.

With the help of Janice Bolinger, an honorary past state regent of the Indiana Daughters of the American Revolution (DAR), we visited the Indiana State Library several times in 2017 and 2018 to look for any pre-1917 information about the flag. We soon discovered that few sources of information existed.

However, in the course of our search, we found that Indiana had two flags, in its past. In 1885, State Librarian Eliza "Lizzie" Callis, a native of Martinsville, was directed by the Indiana General Assembly to create a state flag in time for the formal dedication of the Washington Monument. And, in 1901, lawmakers, in response to a request from Civil War veteran Captain Wallace S. Foster of Indianapolis, adopted "Old Glory" as the state's official flag. (It retained that status until 1988).

Newspaper articles became the major source for tracking any information about the state flag. And, this is how I spent much of my time during the COVID-19 lockdown in 2020 and 2021.

The story of the state flag really began in May 1914 when Irwin Burnett Arnold, a Civil War veteran from Richmond, Indiana, designed a flag with his wife, Lessie, and tried to have the Grand Army of the Republic (GAR) endorse it. They rejected Arnold's flag as did attendees to the state DAR convention in October of that same year.

When the state's Centennial began in 1916, William Chauncy Langdon, a New York-based pageant director, unveiled a flag he created for his pageants in Bloomington, Corydon and Indianapolis. Langdon's design was very similar to Arnold's flag. That same year, the DAR announced it was sponsoring a public flag design contest .They offered a $100 prize for the winning design.

Paul Hadley of Mooresville ultimately was named the winner of the flag design contest. In 1917, lawmakers subsequently approved his entry, but they called it "the state banner," a designation that Hadley's design maintained until 1955.

After closely examining the Arnold, Langdon and Hadley flags, I came to the conclusion that Hadley did not design his flag from scratch. Rather, he either adopted elements of the Arnold and Langdon flags in submitting his contest entry, or, more likely, the state flag proponents hired him to improve on the earlier designs. I subscribe to this latter theory and offer support for my claim in the book's concluding chapter.

The Indiana Flag: Who Really Designed It? is a concise history of the state flag deliberations that took place between 1914 and 1917. Whether you agree with my analysis of what happened, I hope you enjoy reading some previously untold stories about the flag and that the anecdotes presented herein renew your pride in our truly unique state flag.

David B. Reddick

July 2023

CHAPTER ONE

STATE FLAG INITIATIVES, 1914

I n February 1914, Catherine Barlow an official with the National Society of the Daughters of the American Revolution (DAR), wrote a letter to state regents asking them to bring a copy of their state flag to the organization's annual national Congress in Washington, D.C. in April. The plan was to hang the flags in the recently constructed Memorial Continental Hall Auditorium.[1]

Indiana did not have a unique state flag. Not to be embarrassed by the request, Mrs. John Newman (Mary Stewart) Carey of Indianapolis and Mrs. William W. (Julia Meek) Gaar of Richmond, quickly put together an alternative. They presented the DAR Congress with a "bunting flag" upon which they had imprinted the state seal. Before the April meeting concluded, Indiana State Regent Mrs. John (Frances) H. Robertson of Fort Wayne had asked Mrs. Carey to chair a State Flag Committee.[2]

Mary Stewart Carey

Thus began a four-year campaign, largely orchestrated by the DAR, to persuade Indiana lawmakers to adopt a unique state flag. Few written records exist of any flag deliberations that took place even though several patriotic organizations were thought to have participated. As a result, contemporary newspaper accounts were relied heavily upon in telling the flag story.

* * *

Mrs. Carey was an excellent choice to lead the DAR state flag committee. Born March 5, 1859 in Greensburg, Indiana, she and her family moved to Indianapolis in 1863 where her father, Daniel Stewart, became a partner in a wholesale drug business. He later sold his share in the business and operated a successful glass company.[3] After graduating from Mount Vernon Seminary, an exclusive private school for girls in Washington, D.C., Mary Stewart returned home where she married John Newman Carey in 1880.

Carey was a native of Dayton Ohio, whose family also moved to Indianapolis in 1863. After graduating from Brown University, he first worked in the wholesale hardware business before joining the Daniel Stewart Drug Company and later, the Stewart Glass Company. Following Daniel Stewart's passing in 1892, Carey became president of his father-in-law's company. It became known as the Stewart-Carey Glass Company.[4]

As the daughter of a wealthy local family, Mrs. Carey was expected to play an active role within the community. To that end, she soon joined the Indianapolis Woman's Club.[5] It was established in 1875 to "form an organized center for the mental and social culture of its members and for the improvement of domestic life." Mrs. Carey also became a member of the Caroline Scott Harrison and Cornelia Cole Fairbanks DAR chapters. The latter was named for the wife of the 26th Vice President of the United States, Charles W. Fairbanks.[6] Mrs. Carey also actively supported several local charitable causes.[7]

Soon after the DAR Congress ended in April 1914, Mrs. Carey and her committee contacted state DAR chapters and urged them to bring a flag design to the annual state convention in October.[8] More than a dozen entries were received and put on display in the convention hall of the Hotel Anthony in Fort Wayne. One newspaper correspondent covering the meeting noted that the Irwin B. Arnold flag sponsored by the Missisinewa DAR chapter from Portland, Indiana, was "meeting with the most favor and probably will be selected the next day."[9]

Who was the individual behind this apparent winning flag design?

* * *

Irwin Burnett Arnold or I. B. Arnold as he was also known, was born May 6, 1844 in Galena, Ohio, a small village just south of Columbus, the state capital. When Arnold turned 18, he enlisted

Irwin Burnett Arnold

Ad for Arnold's store.

with Company G of the 96th Ohio Infantry. His unit saw action in Mississippi, Arkansas, and Louisiana. Arnold also spent seven weeks as a prisoner of war in Mobile, Alabama, before being released.

After the Civil War ended, Arnold and his brother, Justin, briefly operated a shoe/boot store in Galena before following family members to Champaign, Illinois, where they opened a similar store there.[10] In October 1887, the brothers sold their store and bought a wholesale rubber goods business in Indianapolis.

Two years later, Arnold re-enlisted in the U.S. Army and served in the transportation department in the Philippines during the Spanish-American War. When that conflict ended, Arnold moved to Findlay, Ohio, where he married Lessie May Lindsey Strother. The couple soon moved to Richmond, Indiana, where Arnold became the secretary-treasurer of the Campfield Raggle Block Company. It was owned by his son-in-law, Edwin M. Campfield.[11]

On May 6, 1914, Arnold celebrated his 70th birthday by attending the 35th annual Department of Indiana Grand Army of the Republic (GAR) encampment in Indianapolis, where he spoke in his capacity as the organization's Patriotic Instructor.[12]

Arnold urged his fellow veterans to "keep going" in terms of promoting patriotism among the younger generation even though "you might have passed the summit of usefulness many years ago.[13]

"Let me enjoin you, when talking to children (or to older people, for that matter) to tell incidents, short, trite, truthful stories," Arnold said. "They do not want to hear long, prosy, monotonous history."[14]

In his role as Patriotic Instructor, Arnold said he had given many speeches on the history and evolution of the American flag and had put on display some of the more than 100 flags in his private collection. "No more effective means of cultivating a love of country can be used than the inculcation of a reverence for the flag."[15]

In closing, Arnold mentioned how the Indiana DAR was interested in seeing the state adopt a flag before he showed the veterans the flag that he and his wife, Lessie, had designed.

It had the same color scheme as the Stars and Stripes. The two outer horizontal stripes were red while the middle stripe was white except for a blue pentagon positioned near the hoist. It served as the background for a circle of thirteen stars representing the original colonies. This design element was similar to the iconic Betsy Ross flag.

Five stars representing the states predating Indiana's entry into the Union — Vermont (1791), Kentucky (1792), Tennessee (1796), Ohio (1803), and Louisiana (1812) — were positioned outside the circle. The larger star in the middle of the circle was meant to represent Indiana, the country's nineteenth state. This design feature was similar to a Revolutionary War battle flag carried into the Battle of Cowpens on January 17, 1781.[16]

During the business meeting on the final day of the encampment, Arnold introduced a resolution asking his fellow veterans to support a state flag initiative and to recommend his design to lawmakers. The resolution was met with an immediate, unwelcomed response from past Indiana Commander Orlando A. Somers of Kokomo.

Somers rose from his seat, grabbed an American flag and shouted, "Boys, I move that we adopt the flag that we fought for, and honor and love, as the state flag of Indiana."[17] Most of those in attendance supported Somers and no vote was taken on Arnold's resolution. However, a representative from the Sons of Veterans organization, which had helped to organize the encampment, agreed to appoint a committee and appear before the Indiana General Assembly in 1915 in support of a state flag.[18]

Arnold was undaunted. Over the summer months he approached the Portland, Indiana DAR chapter and persuaded them to support his flag design at the DAR's annual state convention in October. Arnold's design appeared to be the favorite until the morning of the vote when a telegram was received from Secretary of State Lew G. Ellingham of Indianapolis. It informed the delegates that Indiana already had a state flag. Upon hearing this news, the DAR delegates voted to delay selecting a state flag design.[19]

CHAPTER TWO

THE LIBRARIAN'S FLAG, 1885

The Indiana General Assembly opened its 61-day biennial session on January 7, 1915, but without any bills
advocating for a unique state flag.

What had happened to the DAR and the Sons of Veterans?
Both organizations had spoken enthusiastically the year before
about introducing state flag legislation. Perhaps the groups had
underestimated the effort it took to bring a proposal before
legislators.

However, it appears the DAR did not let Secretary of State
Ellingham's telegram discourage them. Mrs. Carey's committee spent part of 1915 learning about the flag mentioned in his
telegram. It was created in 1885 by State Librarian Eliza "Lizzie"
Callis to celebrate the dedication of the Washington Monument.

* * *

Before discussing what led to the librarian's flag, one needs to
be aware of the political climate in the final decades of the nineteenth century. Indiana was the sixth most populist state at the

time and politically, it was considered an important swing state. (A purple state in today's political parlance). As a result, gubernatorial races often were decided by a few thousand votes. House and Senate seats were hotly contested as Democrats and Republicans vied to ultimately control the Indiana General Assembly. Indiana politicians also were encouraged to seek national office.[1]

It was against this backdrop that state lawmakers met on February 2, 1885 and passed Concurrent Resolution No. 6.[2] While concurrent resolutions did not carry the same weight as an enacted law, lawmakers often turned to them when they wished to take a specific action quickly. In this particular case, legislators were responding to a request from the Washington National Monument Society. They were ready to dedicate the long-delayed obelisk honoring George Washington and the Society wanted Indiana to send them a copy of their state flag.[3]

Why were Indiana lawmakers suddenly so interested in this request? Historians have observed how after the Civil War, individuals in Northern states like Indiana developed more patriotic attitudes towards the country as a whole. This often manifested itself with the construction of war-related memorials or by embracing patriotic symbols like the American flag.[4] And, who better to honor in 1885 than George Washington, the father of the country.

★ ★ ★

Eliza "Lizzie" Callis was in her second year as state librarian when she was asked to create a state flag. How she came to find herself in this appointed position is a classic example of the contentious nature of the Democratic and Republican parties at the time.

Eliza "Lizzie" Callis

Callis, one of six children, was born October 19, 1856 in Martinsville to Edwin Willard and Ellen Greene (Orner) Callis. The couple had recently moved to Morgan County from Flemington, New Jersey. Edwin, a printer and bookmaker by trade, purchased the *Morgan County Gazette* in May 1855. At the time, it was considered a Republican publication, but by 1870, Edwin had switched political allegiances and renamed his paper, the *Martinsville Democrat*. Its motto read: "Independent on all Subjects—Neutral on None." Lizzie showed an early interest in her family's newspaper and took control of it, along with her older sister, Anna, when she turned eighteen.[5]

* * *

In 1880, Republican Albert G. Porter of Lawrenceburg became the state's nineteenth Governor after winning the election by seven thousand votes. Democrats despised him. Porter had been a Democrat, but had been ostracized by the party's pro-slavery wing in 1854.[6]

Democrats gained control of the Indiana General Assembly in the 1882 off-year election, winning 59 of the 100 House seats and 28 of the 50 Senate seats.[7] They soon initiated a campaign to stop Porter from making any further political appointments. On January 16, 1883, the Democrats held a caucus meeting in Indianapolis to select their own slate of candidates for state librarian and three prison director positions.

A dozen individuals initially expressed an interest in the state librarian post, but as the caucus meeting drew near, the contest had become a two-woman race between Mrs. T. J. (Mary) Foster of Fort Wayne and Lizzie Callis. Mrs. Foster's husband had been elected to the Indiana House in 1875 and served in the state Senate three years later. He was the former owner of the *Fort Wayne Journal*, but unfortunately took his own life on June 24, 1882.[8]

William Easton English

The road to victory for Callis was not easy. She faced a powerful distractor in William Easton English, an Indianapolis attorney-businessman and a newly elected member of Congress.[9] English had recently assumed management of his father's Opera House and Hotel on Monument Circle in downtown Indianapolis. He and his allies in the Indiana Liquor League opposed any attempts by the Legislature to amend the state Constitution to limit the sale and manufacture of alcoholic beverages.[10]

English believed Callis and her newspaper supported the Constitutional amendment. He stood up at the caucus meeting and said, "I have no interest in any other candidate only it will please me to see Miss Callis rebuked." As one account of the meeting observed, Callis had shown no affinity in her paper for the amendment and "the opposition to Miss Callis, because of his weight and violence, created a sympathy for her."[11]

Mrs. Foster received eighteen first ballot votes to seventeen for Callis. However, Callis surged ahead on the second ballot, winning thirty-nine votes. On the third ballot, Callis won forty-eight ballots — a majority — to become the newest state librarian. She began her job on April 1, 1883 at an annual salary of $1,200.[12]

✳ ✳ ✳

The language of Concurrent Resolution No. 6 directing Callis to create a state flag read as follows:

> *WHEREAS,* it appears that the State of Indiana is now without a State flag, banner or ensign, and

> *WHEREAS,* There has been a request made by the Committee on Arrangements on the dedica-

tion of the Washington Monument, on the 21st of February, 1885, of the State Librarian to furnish one, therefore

Resolved by the House of Representatives, the Senate concurring. That the State Librarian be, and is hereby authorized to purchase a suitable, flag or ensign, and have the Coat of Arms of the State appropriately inscribed thereon.[13]

During debate on the resolution, the *Indianapolis Sentinel* reported that Democratic Senator Inman H. Fowler of Spencer

Monument dedication.

thought the resolution was too broad and a price limit should be attached so the cost was not left entirely to the state librarian.

However, Republican Senator Chester R. Faulkner of Holton came to the librarian's defense: "We

The flag designed by Eliza "Lizzie" Callis.

have a very economical little lady for State Librarian, and I think we had better leave that matter with her. She will get it up in good taste, and one that the State will be proud of, I am satisfied, and not break up the State, either." The Senators ultimately concurred in the resolution.[14]

While it is not known how much Callis spent on the flag, an interesting, unresolved question was how she managed to assemble the flag in less than seventeen days. No records exist as to whether Callis designed the flag herself, had the help of her staff or if she employed someone from outside of state government. What is known is that Callis went well beyond the instructions outlined in the flag resolution.

The state seal that Callis used showed a woodman chopping down a tree to the right of the seal while a woolly buffalo was shown in the foreground jumping over a log. Trees and mountains were featured in the background, but the mountain range was not as pronounced as the seal's modern-day version nor did it show either a sunrise or sunset.

Callis mounted the seal on a blue silk background and embellished its overall image with an oak leaf wreath and a star-spangled shield featuring the original thirteen stars and stripes. The final touches included a red ribbon above the seal with the word "Indiana" spelled out in blue lettering. A gold fringe covered three sides of the flag.[15]

On February 19, Callis sent a note and the flag to Senate President Pro Tem M. D. Manson of Crawfordsville, noting that "it (the flag) is not yet completed, as the center painting is to be removed and the center filled in with embroidery, as shown by the shield, which change will be made as soon as the flag is returned from the Washington Monument Association."[16]

It is believed the flag was returned to Indiana, but its ultimate whereabouts is not known.[17] Likewise, there is no evidence the flag was ever flown in the state.

* * *

When Callis completed her third two-year term in 1889, she returned to Martinsville with her husband, Lieutenant Colonel Jefferson Kingsley Scott, whom she married in December 1887. Scott was born March 27, 1827 in Fayette County, Kentucky, but his family ultimately moved to Martinsville where he was one of the contractors who worked on the first section of the Franklin and Martinsville Railroad.[18]

In 1855, Scott served a four-year term as the Morgan County Circuit Court clerk. During the Civil War, he was a member of both the 7th Indiana Infantry and the 59th Indiana Infantry. Scott saw action in the Corinth, Vicksburg Campaign, the Savannah Campaign, and the Campaign of the Carolinas. After the War, Scott

*Lieutenant Colonel
Jefferson Kingsley Scott*

worked as a hotel manager, an insurance agent and an accountant in Indianapolis.[19]

The couple lived on West Washington Street. Callis volunteered at the Home Lawn Sanatorium, one of several similar sanatoriums that operated in Martinsville at the time. She was a member of the First Presbyterian Church and the Martinsville Woman's Club. She served as its president in 1921 and 1922. Scott, who was 29 years older than his wife, died on April 5, 1903. Callis passed away on September 21, 1923. Both are buried in the Hilldale Cemetery in Martinsville.[20]

CHAPTER THREE

THE PATRIOT'S FLAG, 1901

At the DAR's fifteenth annual conference held in Terre Haute in 1915, Mrs. Carey informed delegates that her committee also learned that on May 15, 1901, the Legislature adopted "Old Glory" as the official state flag.[1] The individual who was most responsible for seeing this law enacted was Wallace Smith Foster, a native of Vernon, Indiana.[2]

Wallace Smith Foster

Foster joined the 9th Indiana Volunteer Infantry on April 12, 1861, the first day of the Civil War. He was not alone. Three of his brothers also enlisted as did 197,141 other Hoosiers, the second highest number of recruits among the Northern states. By the war's end, 25,028 Hoosiers were killed in battle and another 48,568 men were wounded.[3]

Foster first saw action in Cumberland, Maryland, where he served for three months before returning home. In September 1861, Foster then joined the 13th Indiana Volunteer Infantry Regiment as a Lieutenant and spent the next three years, mostly in West Virginia, where he attained the rank of Captain.[4]

When the war ended, Foster became a charter member of the George H. Thomas Post No. 17 of the Grand Army of the Republic (GAR) in Indianapolis. He was appointed to the U.S. Pay Department in Columbus, Ohio, where he secured free transportation and medical help for returning veterans. Unfortunately, he had to retire soon after due to his war-related hearing loss.[5]

In 1882, Foster and Captain Allen G. P. Brown of New York created the Silent Army of Deaf Soldiers, Sailors and Marines organization. The two men submitted a report to Congress in 1890 on the experiences of more than 100 soldiers who suffered total deafness during the Civil War. They argued that these veterans deserved a pension. In 1904, Congress finally agreed and enacted a law giving the deaf veterans a pension of forty dollars a month.[6]

Foster also grew concerned about the influx of immigrants to America, especially from Eastern Europe, and their lack of knowledge of the country's customs and freedoms. In 1890,

Col. George T. Balch

he and Col. George T. Balch of New York, saw a need to teach "American principles" to the immigrants and for developing rituals and practices to foster a sense of American identity. To that end, Balch developed a ritual involving the American flag, along with a pledge and salute, that predated the Pledge of Allegiance. Balch's pledge went as follows: "I *give my heart and my hand to my country—one country, one language, one flag*" [7]

In September 1891, Foster proposed to the National GAR encampment in Detroit that the American flag be raised each day at schoolhouses across the country and on all national patriotic days. Foster tried twice to persuade the GAR veterans to adopt his plan. When veterans ignored him, Foster changed tactics. He approached the Woman's Relief Corps (WRC), the ladies auxiliary of the GAR, who fully embraced his plan. [8]

Before Balch died in 1894, he had produced a four-page folio primer for use by public school teachers. [9] Foster expanded the primer to sixty-two pages and with the help of the WRC, it was distributed to teachers across the country. By 1908, some 50,000 primers; 25,000 facsimiles of the Declaration

Copy of Foster's Primer.

of Independence and 35,000 copies of a publication entitled the "Origins and History of the Stars and Stripes" were given away.[10]

The 45-star flag, 1901.

When the Indiana General Assembly opened its biennial session in 1901, Foster, who had become known as "The Flag Man" for his practice of donating American flags to public schools, was instrumental in having two flag bills introduced.

Senate Bill 239 called for "Old Glory" to become the official flag of Indiana. The bill read as follows:

> *WHEREAS,* The State of Indiana has no flag; and
>
> *WHEREAS,* The flag of the United States is recognized as the flag of every State and Territory composing the United States; therefore,
>
> *SECTION 1. Be it enacted by the General Assembly of the State of Indiana,* That said flag of the United States, representing each State with a star in its blue field, be and is hereby adopted as the flag of the State of Indiana.[11]

House Bill 153, concerned the desecration of the American flag. It provided penalties of $10 for a first offense and not more than $25 for subsequent offenses. It was part of a movement begun in 1897 by several patriotic organizations across the country. They revered the flag and wanted to protect it from "placing any kind of markings, lettering, or pictures on the flag, whether for commercial, political or other purposes." By 1901, eleven states had enacted similar legislation.[12]

Example of a flag desecration.

As one newspaper reported, the presentation of Senate Bill 239 in the House "brought about a wordy war and a display of oratorical pyrotechnics such as have not been heard before in the session." Democratic Minority Leader Cyrus E. Davis of Bloomfield rose from his seat to say: "Notwithstanding the Republican party has raised the flag over the clanking chains of human slaves in the Philippines, Democratic love for the grand old banner is such that we of the minority in this house gladly vote for this bill."[13]

Republican A.M. Scott of Ladoga responded by saying, "We are glad to notice that the Democrats have become so imbued with love of the flag. As we used to say in the army, we have to give a large majority of them a h—l of a thrashing before they were inspired with love." Both bills passed the Legislature. Republican Governor Winfield Durbin of Lawrenceburg signed the flag bill on March 9 and the desecration bill on March 11.[14]

Passage of Senate Bill 239 did not receive much attention from newspaper editors around the state with the exception of a March 16 editorial in the *Columbus Republican.* The paper noted the action taken by lawmakers was "the kind of state rights, that recognizes the sovereignty of the national flag and the unity of all the states into one grand whole." The editorial added: "Indiana has performed a signal service for the whole country in thus adopting the stars and stripes as the flag of the state of Indiana."[15]

An editorial in the May 29th edition of the *Richmond Palladium-Item* also made the following observations about the two bills:

> "It is a curious fact that as late as March 9, 1901, the legislature of this state adopted the American flag as the flag of Indiana. This had either never been thought of before or was thought unnec-

essary. This action was probably taken in order to better enable the state to protect the flag by state law. It was followed by another act by the same legislature, March 11, 1901 "to prevent and punish the improper use and desecration of the flag of the United States." This act is a very stringent law against the use of the American Flag for advertising purposes, making it a serious misdemeanor to place "any words, figures, numbers, marks, inscriptions, pictures design, device, symbol, token, notice, drawing, or any advertisement of any nature" on the flag."[16]

* * *

Foster spent the final years of his life doing what he had done for several years: donating flags to schools and other organizations. He died on March 30, 1919 at his home on Capitol Avenue in Indianapolis from heart disease at the age of eighty-two. In reporting on his death, *The Indianapolis Star* said of him: "Capt. Foster, it may be truly said, lived for the flag. He never lost his zeal for his chosen work and was only hampered in the last year or so by increasing physical disability. He was a truly remarkable character — a man who emphatically did what he could.[17]

***

Mrs. Carey told the DAR convention delegates in Terre Haute in 1915 that the work of her committee "was interrupted last year by the report that the state seal was being used as a banner. This is true, but there is no authority for such use, and the State flag is our flag, as it is obvious that the United States flag belongs to forty-seven other states as well, could not be distinctive nor particularly significant for Indiana."[18]

She offered a resolution asking the delegates to create a public state flag design contest. "No one can question the fertility of the imagination of the Hoosier as shown by the beautiful and numerous designs here submitted. This is too great a proposition not to have all the originality and thought of all Hoosiers."[19]

The resolution was approved unanimously, but an amendment encouraged the committee to collaborate cooperatively with the Grand Army of the Republic.[20]

CHAPTER FOUR

THE CENTENNIAL FLAG, 1916

Six years before Indiana celebrated its 100th anniversary as a state, the General Assembly enacted a law in 1911 to establish the Indiana Centennial Committee.[1] It was composed of representatives from the state's thirteen Congressional districts. The Committee was asked to recommend an appropriate site for a Centennial celebration and to suggest a permanent memorial.

After two years of deliberations, Committee members recommended that the state build a state Library and Museum, noting, "a splendid Library and Museum of the monumental design and fitting environment contemplated, will supply an urgent present need, typifying the patriotic and intelligent spirit of the Commonwealth today; and stand a hundred years hence to proclaim with dignity the high character and citizenship in 1916."[2]

The Committee also called for a celebration "that would typify the history of Indiana in an educational way, especially pageants, which would call the attention of the public to the development and growth of Indiana."[3] This latter recommendation prompted lawmakers to pass a second law in 1915 to create the Indiana Historical Commission (IHC).[4]

The legislation laid out the work of the IHC "to collect, edit and publish documentary and other materials on the history of Indiana" and "to prepare and execute plans for the centennial celebration in 1916."[5] Dr. Frank B. Wynn, an Indianapolis psychiatrist and an early environmental conservationist, was chosen as the Celebration Committee chairman.[6] At a meeting in Corydon in October 1915, Hugh McK. Landon, a prominent Indianapolis banker, recommended that the Committee hire William Chauncy Langdon of New York, president of the American Pageant Association.[7]

William Chauncy Langdon

Langdon was born April 21, 1871 in Florence, Italy. His father, an ordained Episcopal minister, had moved the family there to establish an English-language church for locals and American tourists. The younger Langdon subsequently received an A.B. degree in history from Brown University in 1892 and an A.M. in English the following year.[8]

As historian David Glassberg has observed, Langdon shared the belief "that a historical pageant could offer local townspeople not only novel holiday entertainment and wholesome recreation, but also a stirring experience through which they could visualize solutions to their current social and economic problems."[9]

Langdon viewed historical pageants as "revitalizing rural towns by enabling residents to catch up with history by preserving a version of their traditions, helping them to recognize outmoded practices while promoting a unique local identity, sense of cohesion, and attachment to place."[10]

Soon after arriving in Indiana with his family in the fall of 1915, Langdon discovered the state did not have an officially recognized state flag. To him, the essential requirements for a flag were (1) that it be simple and beautiful; (2) that it contrast yet harmonize with the American flag; (3) that it be of accepted flag design and colors; and (4) that it be significant.[11]

The following is how Langdon described his flag:

> The design of the flag consists of three vertical sections, like the French and Italian flags. The central section is blue, the color of statehood; the two outer sections are green, suggestive of the primeval luxuriance of the wilderness and of the present fertility and productiveness of Indiana. On the central blue field are nineteen golden stars. Thirteen, representing the first thirteen States, are in a circle, in which form they were placed on the first American flag. Five more stars, two in the corners above and three below, repre-

sent the other States which were admitted before Indiana. The star of the nineteenth State is placed in the middle of the circle. The usual gold fringe, emphasizing the essential colors of the flag, completes the design.[12]

Langdon's flag made its debut at the Pageant of Bloomington on May 16, 1916. The three-day event on the campus of Indiana University consisted of "twelve episodes and a finale, in which the historic events will be reproduced by dramatic action, with dialogue, including vivid pantomime, beautiful dances and tableau."[13] A half dozen newspapers in the state printed the following United Press story about the first day of the pageant:

> BLOOMINGTON, Ind., May 16 — More than a thousand men, women and children of Bloomington and students of Indiana University, took part today in the opening of the pageant in celebration of the hundred years of Indiana statehood. The pageant is under the direction of William Chauncey (sic) Langdon, its author. This is but one of many similar celebrations which will be held in scores of Indiana communities this year.[14]

Democratic Governor Samuel M. Ralston of Spencer attended the second day of the pageant along with members of

the Indiana Historical Commission. Ralston took part in the episode depicting the presentation
of the Robert W. Long Hospital
and the Waterman Foundation for
research in the state. The final day
on May 18 was marked by the pageant's largest crowds.[15]

According to *The Indianapolis
News,* "business places in Bloomington were closed and the attendance of Monroe County people
was very large." The Historical Commission reported it had

Gov. Samuel M. Ralston

approved a three-volume set on Indiana history and the design
for the Centennial medal. *The News* also noted that "motion pictures of the entire pageant were taken and the pageant reel will be
preserved by the university." No still pictures of the pageant were
published in any of the newspapers that covered the pageant.[16]

On June 1-2, Langdon's second pageant took place in
Corydon, Indiana, the home of the first state capital.[17] It featured
four episodes: the completion of the territorial courthouse; the
naming of Corydon as the state capital, the 1816 constitutional
convention, and the final episode called the Centennial where all
the characters in the pageant sang the "Hymn to Indiana."[18]

The second day of the pageant drew between 5,000 and 10,000 people. In addition to a repeat of Langdon's production, the day also featured a speech by former Republican Vice President Charles W. Fairbanks of Indianapolis and exhibition drills and folk dances performed by five hundred school children from Evansville.[19]

In a June 4th editorial in *The Indianapolis Star,* the paper noted that "the pageant at Corydon seems to have been an especially successful performance and highly creditable to this historical community, while the speeches were in keeping …Surely a good beginning has been made in the series of celebrations planned by the towns and cities of the state and a high standard set."[20]

Langdon's final and largest pageant, the Pageant of Indiana, featured nine historical episodes and more than 3,000 volunteers. It took place over six days in October at Riverside Park in Indianapolis.[21] More than 4,000 people viewed the opening performance. Crowds continued to grow throughout the week with the largest gathering on Sunday, October 7.[22]

✳ ✳ ✳

Following the end of his Indiana pageants, Langdon returned to New York where he continued to write and produce pageants. In January 1920, he returned to Bloomington to preview a pageant to celebrate the 100th anniversary of Indiana University.[23] The next year, Langdon became a historical librarian for the

American Telephone and Telegraph Company. In 1937, he wrote a social history entitled "Everyday Things in American Life." Langdon died on April 11, 1947 in Westport, Connecticut.[24]

Langdon had a real passion for historical pageants. His papers at the John Hay Library at Brown University show that during his time in Indiana, he often corresponded with several Hoosiers who were producing pageants in their own communities. In all, forty-five pageants were performed throughout Indiana in 1916 with an estimated 250,000 people attending at least one of them.[25]

It is not known from Langdon's papers if he ever communicated with I. B. Arnold about his flag design since the two designs were so similar. Langdon, however, did send a letter, dated May 23, 1916, to Democratic Gov. Samuel M. Ralston of Spencer in which he wished to "offer as a gift to the State of Indiana the flag which I designed for use as the State Flag in the Pageants under my direction at Bloomington, Corydon, and Indianapolis."[26] He also made the same offer to the DAR.

Langdon described in some detail to Gov. Ralston the various aspects of his flag's design and concluded by stating "I shall be glad to hear from you in regard to the acceptability of the design and shall be glad to follow any directions or suggestions you may be so kind as to make."[27]

A side-by-side comparison of the Arnold and Langdon flags show that the only discernable difference between them were

Chauncy Langdon's daughter, Elizabeth, shown holding the flag.

their three panels. Arnold's red and white panels were horizontal while Langdon's blue and green panels were laid out vertically.

Two pictures of Langdon's flag are known to exist. One was published in *The Indianapolis Star* at his Indianapolis pageant. Langdon's daughter, Elizabeth, is shown holding the flag, but it was not unfurled so it was impossible to see the flag's full layout.[28] The second photograph, taken at the same time, showed Elizabeth standing with the unfurled flag in the background while pageant volunteers performed in front of her. The whereabouts of the Arnold and Langdon flags are not known.

* * *

Mrs. Carey and her committee continued their work during 1916. On March 11, they took the first steps towards a public flag design contest, an idea first raised at the annual state DAR conference in 1915 when *The Indianapolis News*, ran a half-page spread announcing the contest.[29] The *News* article featured a photograph of Mrs. Carey surrounded by a montage of nine existing flag designs, including Arnold's flag.

Flag contest announcement in The News *in 1916.*

Each design was subjected to a brief critique, presumably attributable to Mrs. Carey. The critiques seemed intended to inform readers on what the DAR committee considered a suitable flag design. The article also mentioned how Mrs. Carey was offering a $100 award of her own money for the winning entry. The public was given until October 1 to submit their entries.[30]

The DAR article appeared to have the desired effect. Varying accounts suggest that the flag committee received from 100 to 200 entries, including several from Paul Hadley of Mooresville, the declared winner of the flag contest. However, when the October 1 deadline arrived, no design winner was announced. Mrs. Carey offered a reason for the delay when she addressed the DAR's annual conference in Richmond on October 24-25.[31]

"About seventy other banners have been submitted, but at the meeting last Monday, no choice was made. Experts in design were called in, in an advisory capacity," Mrs. Carey said. "They urged the selection of a simple design — simple enough to be recognized at a distance, and simple enough to be printed on a small flag or stamped on a button. It is also desirable to have the colors different from those of the National Emblem. Most of the designs submitted have been too elaborate and not sufficiently striking in symbolism."[32]

Mrs. Carey added that "it is difficult to find a motive to be expressed on our banner, as Indiana has no mountain peak, no great lake or river exclusively its own — but it is possible to find some symbol expressive of its high character and noble history."[33]

CHAPTER FIVE

ENACTING A
STATE BANNER, 1917

W hen the state legislature opened in 1917, it appeared that a bill calling for a state flag might be in jeopardy. Mrs. Carey told the *Indianapo-lis News* on January 5th that the DAR flag design contest would remain open another week.[1]

The *News* article appeared to contradict a report published in October 1916 that described how 11 of 15 patriotic organizations participating in the flag deliberations had chosen Hadley's flag design and their recommendation already had been approved by the state's Adjutant General, Harry B. Smith.[2]

Paul Hadley

"We have some very beautiful designs among the more than 100 submitted," Mrs. Carey told *The Indianapolis News* "but the opportunity is still open, for a week yet, for someone to gain the distinction of and award for, submitting the design that we can take before the legislature."[3]

Mrs. Carey added that while she and her committee had been at work on a state flag for two years, "we have not yet the simplicity that is so desirable. There is not yet the lofty symbolism and simplicity."[4]

She encouraged competitors to come forth with their ideas within the next week and reiterated what her group sought in a design entry.

"The banner or flag must, of course, be original, direct, bold and simple. It must be clearly symbolized of Indiana or express a high ideal suitable for adoption. Designs that can be reproduced easily, and cheaply, naturally will have preference. Only the strong primary colors — and only a limited number of these — are used in most of the distinctive and beautiful flags and banners."[5]

Had Paul Hadley not submitted his winning design yet, or was he sent back to the drawing board to tweak his design? Whatever "outstanding" issues were present on January 5th apparently were soon resolved.

On February 13, Democratic freshman Senator Abraham Simmons of Bluffton introduced Senate Bill 344 to adopt a state flag.[6] It was forwarded to the Soldiers and Sailors Committee chaired by Republican Senator Harry E. Negley of Indianapolis.

His Committee subsequently amended both sections of the bill, removing the phrase "state flag" and substituting it with the phrase "state banner." The second section had called for the repeal of the American flag as the flag of Indiana. Instead, Section 1 of the revised bill now read:

> "Section 1. Be it enacted by the General Assembly of the State of Indiana, That a State Banner is hereby adopted, and the same shall be of the following design and dimensions, to-wit: Its dimensions shall be five (5) feet and six (6) inches fly by four (4) feet and four (4) inches hoist, and the field of the same shall be blue with nineteen (19) stars and a flaming torch in gold or buff. Thirteen (13) stars shall be arranged in an outer circle and representing the original thirteen states, five (5) stars in a half circle below the torch and inside the outer circle of stars, and representing the States admitted prior to Indiana, and the nineteenth (19th) star, appreciably larger than the others and representing Indiana, placed above the flame of the torch. The outer circle of stars so arranged that one star shall appear directly in the middle at the top of the circle, and the word: "Indiana," to be

placed in a half circle over and above the star representing Indiana and midway between it and the star in the center above it. Rays to be shown radiating from the torch to the three (3) stars on each side of the star in the upper center of the circle."[7]

The amended second section now read: "Section 2. The banner described in Section 1 hereof, shall be regulation in addition to the American flag, with all of the militia forces of the State of Indiana, and in all public functions in which the State may or shall officially appear."[8]

The bill passed the Senate unanimously before it was forwarded to the House where it was approved 63 to 15 votes. Newly elected Republican Governor James P. Goodrich of Winchester, a Civil War veteran, let Senate Bill 344 become law on May 11, 1917 without his signature.[9]

After four years of effort, Mrs. Carey's committee and the other patriotic organizations had succeeded in seeing Indiana adopt a unique state banner. Now, the question was whether the public would embrace it.

✳ ✳ ✳

Weeks before the Indiana banner was adopted, Democratic President Woodrow Wilson appeared before a joint session of Congress on April 2, 1917 and asked them for a declaration of war against Germany. Four days later, Congress gave the President the necessary authorization to enter World War I.

Efforts were soon under way across the country to recruit young men for the war effort. By the end of April, Indiana already ranked third among the states with 187 signed recruits.[10] By May, that number had grown to 4,989, just shy of the state's quota of 5,400 recruits.[11] In all, some 130,000 Hoosiers served in World War I. More than 3,000 of them became casualties of the war.[12]

Two days after President Wilson addressed Congress, several prominent Indianapolis residents sent telegrams to their Congressional representatives asking them not to support the country's entry into the war. Typical of these so-called "peace" telegrams was one sent by Otto N. Frenzel, president of Merchants National Bank. "Trust you may see your way clear to keep us out of the war. With sincere loyalty to our President and country." Another "peace" telegram was said to have come from Mrs. Carey.[13]

While Mrs. Carey may have personally opposed the war, she had already begun to do her part even before the President's war declaration. In February 1917, she urged her DAR colleagues "to join the Red Cross immediately by taking out a membership and indicating to the Red Cross what you can do, and further indicate that you are joining as a member from our organization… the Indiana Daughters of the American Revolution are ready and anxious to serve their country, through the Red Cross, by every means within our power and capacity."[14]

Paul Hadley probably opposed the war as well given his Quaker background, but it did not stop him from joining several prominent Indiana artists in creating posters for the U.S. Navy and the comforts committee of the Navy League.[15]

At some point in 1917, Mrs. Carey and Hadley met to produce a proper state banner. Hadley had glued the torch and stars of his initial banner design because he could not find anyone to stitch everything together for him.

Years later, Hadley recalled how he and Mrs. Carey visited the L.S. Ayres Department Store in downtown Indianapolis where they selected the correct colors and appropriate silk fabric to make a proper banner.[16]

Once the flag was finished, Mrs. Carey unveiled it in October in front of her colleagues at the DAR's annual meeting in Indianapolis. Delegates also learned that funds had been raised to purchase an ambulance for troops stationed in France and the vehicle would be marked with the U.S. flag and the Indiana state banner.[17]

In December, Mrs. Carey presented the state banner to Mrs. R.C. Bennett, chairman of the Indianapolis branch of the Navy League.[18] She forwarded the flag to the commander of the USS Indiana (BB-1), the first battleship built in 1893 for the U.S. Navy.

USS Indiana

Commander Anthony F. Nicklett responded to Mrs. Bennett in January, thanking her for the fifteen Christmas comfort bags sent to the men aboard his ship as well as the state banner.[19] The banner ultimately was returned to Indiana after the war and spent several years on display at The Children's Museum of Indianapolis before it was given to the Indiana State Museum.[20]

CHAPTER SIX

THE BANNER YEARS, 1917-1955

As Indiana entered the 1920s, an editorial writer for *The Indianapolis Star* wondered at length what had happened to the state banner since its enactment in 1917. "The flag is not to be found in the Statehouse, and the inquirer at the state library is referred to a picture postcard, which shows the design in black and white, with a printed description."[1] The writer then added:

> "This neglect of a state emblem is an example of our American tendency to go a certain distance with a movement and then to stop before its final accomplishment, either from inertia or because our attention is distracted by something which for the moment seems more interesting or more important. If it was considered fitting in 1916 that Indiana should follow the example of many of her sister states and adopt a flag, someone in authority should see that this flag should be manufactured

and should be displayed on all suitable occasions together with the flag of the United States."[2]

The editorial writer raised some valid points. A few newspaper stories described how DAR chapters around the state had received banners and how one was displayed in Goshen to mark the oldest water mill in Indiana.[3] There was little evidence the banner was being produced in any great quantities. This point was underscored in November 1923 when Mrs. Henry A. Beck of Indianapolis was named chairman of a DAR committee to investigate the manufacture and distribution of the state banner.[4] That same year, though, a state banner was delivered to the U.S. Postal Department in Washington, D.C. where it was included with twenty-nine other state flags on display in the Department's head office.[5]

As for displaying the flag, Republican State Representative Elizabeth Rainey addressed that question during the 1923 session of the Indiana General Assembly. Rainey, the first Marion County female representative elected to the Legislature (Mrs. Julia Nelson of Muncie was the first female elected in 1920) introduced Concurrent Resolution No. 6 "requiring the superintendent of buildings and grounds to see to it that the state flag (banner) hangs below the national colors from the staff of the Statehouse dome."[6]

Perhaps the most "exposure" the state banner received in the 1920s came on December 11, 1925 when the Indiana Historical

Bureau distributed thousands of prints of the banner to school children throughout the state. The Bureau was marking the 109th anniversary of Indiana becoming the 19th state.[7] DAR chapters also continued to actively promote the state banner in the latter half of the 1920s and into the early 1930s by donating banners, for instance, to public schools in Lafayette or giving them away as prizes for academic achievement.[8]

* * *

With enactment of the state ban-ner behind her, Mrs. Carey turned her attention to two other civic projects. She donated her fam-ily's Indianapolis homestead at 5050 North Meridian Street to the Orchard School, a progressive school for elementary school-aged

1150 North Meridian Street

students. In addition to the house providing plenty of classroom space, the property also featured a large orchard in the backyard where children could explore the wonders of nature.[9]

While on a trip to New York in 1925, Mrs. Carey visited the Brooklyn Children's Museum. She was so taken with the facil-ity that upon her return home, she convened a meeting of civic leaders which led to the formation of The Children's Museum of Indianapolis. The Museum initially occupied space behind the

Propylaeum on North Delaware Street before it moved in 1926 to the shelter house in Garfield Park.[10] The following year, Mrs. Carey turned over her own Indianapolis home at 1150 North Meridian Street to the Museum's board of directors.[11]

Mrs. Carey did not live long enough to see the Museum move to its present location on North Illinois Street. She died on June 14, 1938, but her memory lives on today not only through the Children's Museum and the Orchard School, but also as the woman primarily responsible for the Indiana state banner.[12]

* * *

Union Trust building.

Paul Hadley's career began to blossom in the 1920s. He rented a fifth-floor studio in the Union Trust Building at 120 East Market Street in 1921.[13] That fall, Hadley spent three months in Europe, painting in Italy, Switzerland, France, Belgium, and England. Upon his return, some of his watercolors were exhibited at the Woman's Department Club.[14] The next year, Hadley joined the faculty of the John Herron Art Institute in Indianapolis as an interior decorating instructor.

Hadley's artwork soon began to win accolades. In 1923, he won first place in the fine-art category at the Indiana State Fair

as well as the "most popular" prize.[15] That
same year, students at John Herron, real-
izing there was no state banner inside the
state Capitol, created one and presented it
to the state.[16] In March 1924, Hadley had
an exhibit at the Art Institute. He closed
out the decade in 1929 by being named a
watercolor instructor at Herron.[17]

Paul Hadley

* * *

Hadley's fortunes and those of other Indiana artists changed
dramatically in the 1930s. The Art Association of Indianapolis, faced with a declining student enrollment and lost revenue
due to the Great Depression, announced in May 1933 that it had
hired Donald Magnus Mattison, a 28-year-old New York painter
to become the new Dean of the Herron Art Institute.[18]

Less than two weeks later, Mattison fired eight of Herron's
fifteen instructors, including Hadley, who fared better than some
of his colleagues. He became the assistant curator of the museum
side of the Herron Art Institute. He was also commissioned to
design a series of benches in the Indiana Building at the Century of Progress Exhibition in Chicago. By the end of the decade,
Hadley had given up his Indianapolis art studio, but he continued to paint, mostly from his home in Mooresville.[19]

* * *

As Indiana moved into the 1940s, the public's attention soon focused on the country's entry into World War II. Once again, Hoosiers were quick to answer the call to duty with 338,000 men and 118,000 women volunteering to serve.[20]

While a few recruits may have taken a state banner with them into battle, Charles T. Hodgson of South Bend showed how average Hoosiers were beginning to appreciate the importance of the state banner.

Hodgson, a machinist, was sent to Hawaii soon after the Japanese attacked Pearl Harbor. In a letter to Democratic Governor Henry F. Schricker of North Judson, Hodgson described how he lived in a facility with guys from Michigan, who brought along their state flag to hang on the wall of their living quarters. Hodgson asked Schricker if he could send him an Indiana state banner. The Governor, perhaps sensing an opportunity for a brief respite from the furious battles he was having with Republican majorities in the House and Senate, sent Hodgson a banner and an autographed picture of himself.[21]

Paul Hadley was in his 60s when World War II began, but he showed no signs of slowing down. He continued to have gallery exhibits in places like South Bend and in Indianapolis at the H. Lieber Gallery. It was during one of those exhibits in 1947 that Lucille E. Morehouse, long-time art critic of *The Indianapolis Star*, made the following observation of Hadley's artwork:

When Paul Hadley does landscape painting in watercolors, he puts so much personal charm into his work that it might easily impress gallery visitors as entirely creative. As a matter of fact, it is realism of the finest type. His trees have character — there's no mistaking a willow for an oak nor a maple tree for a sycamore.[22]

* * *

Military personnel serving overseas continued to ask state officials for a banner. In July 1951, Secretary of State Republican Leland L. Smith of Logansport took down the state banner hanging in his office and sent it to Corporal Robert G. Long of South Bend.

Long, who was stationed in Hokkaido, Japan, wanted to hang the banner in the chow hall alongside flags from Oklahoma and Michigan.[23] In November, the *Huntington Herald-Press* sent a banner to hometown Private First-Class Edman R. Camomile serving in Korea.[24]

The next year, Mrs. Carl Gates, president of the Robison-Ragsdale American Legion Auxiliary, came to the aid of the *Indianapolis News* after they received a request for a state banner from another U.S. serviceman serving in Korea, Private First-Class Bobby Pyland of Indianapolis.[25]

To its credit, the Indiana Department of Corrections had begun having inmates at the Indiana State Prison in Michigan City make state banners, and later, inmates at the Women's Prison in Indianapolis, but the demand for the banners was now outstripping production.[26]

CHAPTER SEVEN

HADLEY'S STATE FLAG, 1955-2016

When the 89th biennial session of the Indiana General Assembly opened in January 1955, Senators Charles F. Rutledge of Elwood and Donald M. Ream of Indianapolis both indicated their willingness to introduce legislation to have the state banner become the state's official flag.[1]

What was motivating these Republican senators to change the status of Paul Hadley's banner after thirty-eight years? One theory held that state legislators, out of respect for the state's Civil War veterans, had been reluctant to change the status of Hadley's banner until the last veteran had died. That occurred in February 1949 when John C. Adams of Jonesboro passed away at the age of 101.[2]

Another reason may have been to help Republican Governor George N. Craig of Brazil in the eyes of his fellow veterans. Craig was a trial attorney who served as Governor from 1953 to 1957.

He was viewed as a progressive Republican and was not universally liked by many of his GOP colleagues, especially the state's two more conservative U.S. Senators, Homer E. Capehart and William E. Jenner.

Craig had served in the European theatre during World War II and was the first veteran from that war to become commander of the American Legion (1949-1950). He also was the first World War II veteran elected Governor. Senator Rutledge was considered one of Craig's strongest political allies.[3]

Whatever the reason, Senate Bill 47, the Rutledge-Ream bill, was introduced on January 11th and referred to the Committee on Federal Relations, where it was reported out of committee a week later. When it came before the full Senate on January 27th, senators voted 46 to 1 in favor of the bill.[4]

Senate Bill 47 provided a choice in the flag's design and dimensions. The flag could now be five feet fly, by three feet hoist or three feet fly by two feet hoist. The bill also directed "township trustees, boards of school trustees and boards of school commissioners of various school corporations of this state, and board of county commissioners of the several counties of the state, may procure a state flag for each school and for each courthouse under their respective supervision and cause the same to be placed conspicuously in the principal room or assembly hall and any courtroom of any such building or courthouse."[5]

Now that Hadley's design was officially recognized as the Indiana state flag, the obvious question was whether the instructions to certain governmental entities on how to display the flag would be followed and would passage of the bill cause more Hoosiers to embrace and fly the flag.

* * *

As Indiana moved into the 1960s, three major celebrations helped to change Hoosier attitudes towards Paul Hadley's flag. The first event was the state's Sesquicentennial in 1966. During the 94th biennial session of the Indiana General Assembly in 1965, both legislative chambers approved House Concurrent Resolution 18 which read in part that the Sesquicentennial "should include widespread displays of the State Flag of Indiana throughout the State."[6]

On March 2, Senate Concurrent Resolution 21 honored Hadley by stating "in connection with the observation of the Sesquicentennial Celebration in 1966, [the Senate] does hereby honor and commend Mr. Paul Hadley, an octogenarian citizen of the State of Indiana, for his brilliant and perceptive work in designing the official flag of the State of Indiana."[7]

The Sesquicentennial celebrations kicked off on April 16, 1966 when Democratic Governor Roger D. Branigin of Lafayette, with help from Deputy Postmaster General Frederick C. Belen, officially unveiled Indiana's Sesquicentennial stamp in a ceremony at Corydon, the home of the first state capital.[8] Branigin also used the occasion to urge Hoosiers to rededicate themselves to "the high purposes of patriotism, morality and hard work."[9]

Paul Wehr of Indianapolis, a commercial artist, won the stamp's design competition. His entry was selected from more than a hundred entries received in January 1966.[10]

Sesquicentennial stamp.

Also named as the official emblem of the Sesquicentennial Commission, the stamp was vertical in design with blue, yellow, and brown colors. The lower half of the stamp featured a map of the state in blue into which was inset the Indiana torch and a cluster of 19 brown stars, based on Hadley's state flag design. Above the map in a brown circle, "Sesquicentennial 1816-1966" appeared in blue. Bisecting the circle horizontally with the word "Indiana" in white, above which the old capitol building at Corydon also appeared in a white outline. At the bottom of the stamp in brown were the words "U.S. Postage" and the denomination "5¢" also in brown at the lower right corner. The background of the stamp was yellow. The Postal Service ordered 115 million stamps to be printed. Corydon Postmaster Walter A. Fried said he had hired extra help to process the first day cover requests that he anticipated receiving at his post office.[11]

The Sesquicentennial celebrations went a long way to raise the profile of Hadley's state flag, but there were other signs it was gaining more public acceptance, For instance, the *Bedford Daily-Times Mail* undertook a campaign in 1962 to sell miniature versions of the state flag (12 by 18 inches) for one dollar apiece. The newspaper also offered three by five-foot versions of the Stars and Stripes for three dollars and urged readers to buy the flags in advance of that year's Fourth of July celebrations.[12] The *Muncie Evening Press* also promoted a similar flag campaign in 1967 to honor President Lincoln's birthday.[13]

Hadley flag for sale in Bedford paper.

* * *

In 1971, as the United States soon prepared to celebrate the country's 200th birthday, the Indiana General Assembly enacted a law creating the Indiana American Revolution Bicentennial Committee (IARBC). In November, Republican Governor Edgar D. Whitcomb of Jennings County named eleven committee members, including former Democratic Governor Roger D. Branigin of Lafayette, as its chairman.[14] Unfortunately, Branigin had to step down in May 1975 due to ill health (he died that November).

Former Republican state senator Walter P. Helmke of Fort Wayne assumed Branigin's role.[15] As well, Michelle A. White, a Ball State University administrator, was named the Committee's latest executive director in August 1975.[16] Despite these late appointments, the IARBC was successful in undertaking statewide projects to celebrate the country's Bicentennial. For example, on November 20, 1975, the George Rogers Clark Trail was dedicated in Vincennes.[17] The Committee also commissioned a book written by George Waller, a Butler University history professor, on "The American Revolution in the West."[18]

The IARBC also offered Hoosiers the opportunity to purchase a commemorative medal featuring a profile of George Rogers Clark on one side and the seal of Indiana on the other side. Initially, the offering was for either a silver or bronze version of the medal, but the federal government gave the IARBC permission to sell an 18-karat gold version as well.[19]

Chairman Helmke announced in late 1975 that the IARBC had amassed more than $500,000 in state and federal funds to celebrate the country's Bicentennial. Committees were encouraged to submit plans for their Bicentennial festivities. They could be eligible for grants up to $2,500. Helmke said that 280 city and county Bicentennial communities had submitted proposals.[20]

As July 4th approached, activities were underway across the state. For example, on July 2nd, a time capsule was sealed at the Kokomo courthouse and a family concert was held in Pendleton.[21] A hot air balloon was launched on July 4th from the northside of the Indiana statehouse. Throughout the day, visitors could sign a document reaffirming the principles of the Declaration of Independence. The scrolls became part of a permanent display at the state capitol.[22]

The U.S. Postal Service did its part to promote the Indiana state flag in 1976 with a special commemorative stamp program featuring state flags from all 50 states.[23] And, the National Park Service in South Dakota also

U.S. Bicentennial stamp, 1976.

played a small role by flying the Indiana flag in a special Flags of Mount Rushmore program.[24]

The final state Bicentennial project came on December 20th when several dignitaries joined Republican Governor Otis R.

Bowen of Bremen in dedicating a time capsule and the scrolls signed on July 4th. The time capsule was encased in a wall on the first floor of the Statehouse and was not to be opened until 2075.[25]

* * *

Indiana Bicentennial flag.

The third celebration to solidify the Indiana state flag was the state's Bicentennial in 2016. It kicked off on Statehood Day, December 11, 2015, when Republican Governor Mike Pence of Columbus entertained 1,200 fourth graders in the Statehouse rotunda.[26] A special white flag was unveiled for the state Bicentennial. It featured an outline of the state in blue with the state flag torch inset in the state image. This was like the Sesquicentennial stamp design. An outer circle surrounding the state map included the words "Celebrating 200 Years" and contained six stars. A total of 660 flags were distributed to governmental entities around the state.[27]

Each county was urged to appoint a county coordinator to work with local groups to create projects to celebrate the Bicentennial. To help promote these events, the Bicentennial Commission created a program where events could be officially recognized as state Legacy projects. Some 1,650 projects were ultimately approved.[28]

The Bicentennial's capstone event — a Torch Relay event — traveled throughout each of the state's 92 counties. It began September 9 in Corydon and finished October 15 in front of the Statehouse in downtown Indianapolis. It covered 3,200 miles and involved more than 2,000 volunteers who carried the torch.[29]

Torch Relay Logo.

The book's next chapter looks at how the town of Mooresville embraced its adopted son, Paul Hadley, and how the town became known as the Home of the State Flag.

CHAPTER EIGHT

MOORESVILLE'S LOVE AFFAIR
WITH PAUL HADLEY

Mooresville's love affair with Paul Hadley really began in 1902 when he and his family first moved to this northern Morgan County community. Paul, the youngest of four sons of Evan and Ella Quinn Hadley, was born in Indianapolis on August 5, 1880.

He attended Indianapolis High School (later renamed Shortridge High School) but left after his freshman year to study at Manual Training High School (later renamed Emmerich Manual High School) under the direction of Otto Stark, one of the Hoosier Group artists.[1] After graduating from high school, Paul enrolled at the prestigious Pennsylvania Museum and School of Industrial Design in Philadelphia in 1900.[2]

In late 1902, however, Paul returned home to help build a small house for his parents on West South Street. (The house was later moved to 320 Lockerbie Street and still stands today). Paul's father, Dr. Evan Hadley, was born and raised in the Bethel neighborhood southwest of Mooresville before he attended Earlham College in Richmond and the Medical College of Indiana. He ran a successful private medical practice in Indianapolis for more than 30 years before relinquishing it due to ill health.

Evan Hadley died in May 1903, only months after the family had moved.[3] Soon after his father's passing, Paul returned to Philadelphia, where he took a one-semester class in beginning drawing at the Pennsylvania Academy of the Fine Arts before working for a company that designed stained-glass windows. He also worked a few years as an interior designer in Chicago before returning to Mooresville for good in 1912 to help care for his mother, Ella, and his oldest brother, Evan, who was developmentally disabled.[4]

Hadley supported himself by doing private design work for wealthy local residents, including a stained glass window for Indianapolis author Booth Tarkington's summer home in Maine. Tarkington was a first cousin of Mrs. John Carey.[5]

Close friends and family described Hadley as a tall, erect man with white hair. He was a quiet, modest and dignified person who often delighted his friends with an unexpected bit of quick humor. Hadley loved nature and enjoyed taking long walks in the country. Those walks often became the inspiration for his watercolors. He was a member of the Mooresville Nature Club and Mooresville Friends Church.[6]

* * *

Hadley never spoke too often about winning the DAR state flag design contest, but in one interview, he acknowledged the inspiration for the torch had come both from the figure atop the Soldiers and Sailors Monument in downtown Indianapolis and the Statue of Liberty in New York City. The torch in Hadley's design was meant to represent liberty and enlightenment and the six rays were to represent their far-reaching influence. He said individuals who made copies of his flag often positioned the lower two rays downward.[7]

* * *

Rebecca "Becky" Hardin is considered the individual most responsible for persuading her fellow residents to honor Paul Hadley's achievement as the designer of the state flag. Hardin was born in nearby Monroe Township on September 1, 1908.

Rebecca "Becky" Hardin

Soon after graduating from Mooresville High School in 1927, she worked for twenty years as a secretary at the Allison Division of General Motors and then for fifteen years as a file clerk with the federal Small Business Administration in Indianapolis.[8]

During much of that time, Hardin was also a part-time correspondent with the *Mooresville Times* and then the *Martinsville Reporter* when the two newspapers merged. Hardin wielded considerable influence through her weekly column called "Becky's Bit." Like Hadley, Hardin never learned to drive an automobile so she often advocated for more sidewalks to be built around town.[9]

Her friendship with Paul Hadley was cemented during their daily trips to work in Indianapolis on the Interurban Railroad. Hardin is thought to have persuaded the Mooresville Consolidated School Corporation to announce in July 1965 that it was naming its new junior high school, still under construction, after Hadley (it was later renamed Paul Hadley Middle School). In November of that same year, the Mooresville Town Council announced that it was adopting the slogan "the Home of the State Flag." The Chamber of Commerce soon erected a sign with that slogan along State Road 67.[10]

The following spring, the Paul Hadley Junior High School was formally dedicated. Unfortunately, Hadley no longer lived in Mooresville. After his mother, Ella, died in 1930, Hadley and his older brother, Evan, sold the family's two-story house at 2 West South Street in 1950. The family had lived there since 1907. The brothers then moved into a smaller house at 24 East Washington Street until Evan died in 1954. (The house was subsequently demolished and is now part of the parking lot for Citizens Bank).[11]

In 1956, Hadley, who still did not drive, moved into a small apartment at 115 North East Street in Plainfield so he could be on a regular bus line to Indianapolis. Six years later, Hadley moved to Cincinnati, Ohio, to live with relatives of his older brother, Chalmers, the retired director of the Cincinnati Public Library.[12] In June 1969, Hadley moved into the Reid Memorial Nursing Home in Richmond, Indiana to be closer to the family of another older brother, Harvey, a retired physician.

Hadley died on January 31, 1971 at the age of 90.[13] A few days later, the Indiana Senate passed a resolution acknowledging Hadley's passing and referring to him as "the dean of Hoosier watercolor artists."[14]

✳ ✳ ✳

As America prepared to celebrate the country's Bicentennial in 1976, Rebecca Hardin self-published a biography of Paul Hadley.[15] Hardin spent more than $3,000 of her own money to produce her biography. The book also attempted to catalogue Hadley's many watercolor paintings. Hardin planned to donate any "profits" to a local scholarship in the artist's name once she recouped her own costs.[16] She died on July 20, 1995.[17]

✳ ✳ ✳

In 2016, Mooresville and Morgan County actively took part in the state's Bicentennial. Several Legacy events were approved by the state. They included a Flag Town 5K Run and Walk in Mooresville sponsored by the Lambda Nu Chapter of Delta Theta Tau; the Waverly Park dedication and a large county map project.

The Morgan County Leadership Academy raised $10,000 to see that a copy of the map was placed in every school in the county while the Morgan County History and Genealogy Association supplied the information printed on the maps.[18]

Two years prior to the state's Bicentennial, the Mooresville Redevelopment Commission, undertook a three-phase Gateway and Corridor Project to help promote the town as the home of the state flag. Phase I involved construction of two identical monuments north and south of the town limits along State Road 67. The monuments featured a limestone topographical map of the state along with a torch and a brick wall showing Mooresville as the home to the state flag. The final part of the first phase featured a 60-foot-high obelisk with a nine-foot flame at the corner of State Road 67 and Indiana Street.

Mooresville Gateway Monument.

Paul Hadley Bicentennial Park

Phase II focused on widening Indiana Street from State Road 67 to Main Street with a median down the center of the road. The final phase turned a parking lot at Main and Indiana Streets previously owned by Citizens Bank into the Paul Hadley Bicentennial Park.[19]

Not everyone in Mooresville favored the Redevelopment Commission's plans. Much of the opposition centered on the $12 million bond floated to help pay for the projects and other initiatives undertaken in town. Several residents became upset when the nighttime lighting of the flames initially did not work and the landscaping at the monument sites often flooded.

Merchants along Indiana Street also objected to the lack of access to their businesses during construction of the corridor.

Residents and some downtown merchants became angry at losing parking spaces for the Bicentennial Park. In the end, the projects were completed and many residents began to enjoy summer music concerts held at Bicentennial Park.[20]

One of the town's Legacy projects focused on a series of activities held at the Mooresville Public Library during 2016. Beginning in February, Library director Diane Huerkamp and her staff sponsored a five-part Famous Mooresvillians lecture series. It featured presentations on town founder, Samuel Moore; baseball legend, Amos Rusie; and two adopted sons, Frank Inn, a well-known Hollywood animal trainer and Sammy Davis, a Congressional Medal of Honor recipient; as well as a panel discussion on Paul Hadley.

The Library also expanded its existing display of Hadley artwork when former Mooresville resident, Sam Carlisle, loaned part of his collection of Hadley paintings. The final touch to the Hadley display was the template the artist used to create his design. In 2000, it was given to the town's Academy Museum (now defunct) after a couple in Richmond, Indiana found it in a barn among some of Hadley's books and other possessions.[21]

Two other events took place in 2016 that involved Hadley. In June, a dedication ceremony honoring the artist took place at Crown Hill Cemetery in Indianapolis. A flagpole and a simple marker were placed near his gravestone. Charles "Bud" Swisher, a member of the Celebrate Mooresville Committee, spoke briefly at the ceremony about Hadley's artwork.[22] A second dedication involving the unveiling of the Paul Hadley/Indiana State Flag Historical Marker, was held August 6 in downtown Mooresville.[23] (See Appendix A for photos and the wording of the historical marker).

Among the dignitaries who spoke at the marker ceremony were Casey Pfeiffer, the historical program manager for the Indiana Historical Bureau; Keith Lindauer, president and CEO of Citizens Bank; Lois Huntington, State Regent of the Indiana Daughters of the American Revolution; Charles "Bud" Swisher of Healthier Morgan County; and Janice Bolinger, Honorary State Regent, Indiana DAR, who related the history of the Hadley flag. Funds for the historical marker were provided by Citizens Bank and the Indiana DAR.[24]

CHAPTER NINE

WHO REALLY DESIGNED
THE STATE FLAG?

For years, Indiana school children have been taught that Paul Hadley of Mooresville designed the state flag and won $100 in prize money for his efforts. But, is that what really happened? After conducting the research for this book, I don't believe so. The following set of facts supports my alternate theory on what truly happened.

Hadley and Herron student Ralph Priest working on flag.

Three men — Irwin Burnett Arnold, William Chauncy Langdon and Paul Hadley — designed potential state flags between 1914 and 1917, but only Arnold was considered a flag expert. When he learned early in 1914 that the Indiana DAR was considering a state flag, Arnold and his wife quickly designed a flag that mirrored the Stars and Stripes. It had the familiar red, white and blue color scheme as well as a circle of stars representing the country's first thirteen states, much like the iconic Betsy Ross flag. The large star in the center of the circle was meant to represent Indiana, the country's nineteenth state.

The Richmond resident deserves full marks for the uniqueness of his pentagon-shaped canton. However, in my opinion, his biggest design "flaw" was the randomness of the five stars representing the states preceding Indiana's entry into the Union. Their placement did not make for a unified design.

Arnold's design may well have become the state flag if not for two untimely events. Arnold totally misjudged his fellow Civil War veterans and their undying loyalty to "Old Glory" at the GAR encampment in May 1914. His second "mistake" was being unaware of the state flag "created" in 1885 to honor the dedication of the Washington Monument. Had that flag not been revealed in October 1914, the DAR probably would have chosen Arnold's design and lobbied for its enactment with lawmakers in 1915.

William Chauncy Langdon's role in the flag design debate was completely different. His involvement was really one of "convenience" and "opportunity." Hired by the state in late 1915 to produce Centennial pageants in Bloomington, Corydon and Indianapolis, Langdon soon appropriated Arnold's flag design, making only modest changes to it. He moved Arnold's canton to the center of his flag, drawing more attention to the configuration of stars. He also used only two colors compared to Arnold's three-color combination. However, Langdon's two outer green vertical panels did not make much sense. His explanation that they represented "the primeval luxuriance of the wilderness" seemed condescending to me.

Rather than proceed to an analysis of Paul Hadley's flag design, it may be more appropriate to first examine the actions taken by Mrs. John Newman Carey and her State Flag Committee. After learning about the the 1885 flag, Mrs. Carey and her group were left to completely start over again rather than to prepare a bill for lawmakers to consider in January 1915.

As a result, the DAR spent much of that year researching the origin of the Washington Monument flag and the decision in 1901 to make the Stars & Stripes the official flag of Indiana. This latter realization infuriated Mrs. Carey. She thought it presumptuous of lawmakers to think the national flag was special to only Hoosiers and not the rest of the country. At its state convention in October, the DAR agreed to conduct a public flag design contest and to work collaboratively with the GAR.[1]

As the state's Centennial celebrations began in 1916, the DAR announced its flag design contest in March. The half-page newspaper article spelled out what the Committee was looking for in a suitable flag design. Mrs. Carey even offered $100 of her own money for the winning entry.[2]

However, a winner was not announced as planned at the organization's state convention in October. Mrs. Carey explained that most entries were "too elaborate and not surprisingly striking in symbolism." She said part of the problem was because Indiana lacked a unique physical symbol like a mountain peak, great lake or river but added, "it is possible to find some symbol expressive of its high character and noble history."[3]

When the Legislature opened on January 4, 1917, a unique state flag bill had not yet been introduced. In a newspaper article published the following day, Mrs. Carey announced the DAR's design contest would remain open another week. She admitted her group had "not yet found the lofty symbolism and simplicity" they desired.[4] A bill was subsequently introduced in the Senate on February 13th.

The sequence of events described above is important, I believe, because it helps to explain when and how Paul Hadley became involved in the state flag design. One article I found mentioned how a majority of patriotic organizations favored Hadley's flag design at the time of the 1916 DAR convention. However, it was written in 1972 and ignored the fact that the convention's minutes did not mention Hadley's design being finalized.[5]

Instead, what the minutes showed is that a discussion took place among some design experts prior to the convention wherein they offered their advice on what would constitute a good design. The minutes also revealed that Irwin Burnett Arnold was one of the experts in attendance.[6] He must have spoken convincingly about the rationale of his design elements because they are clearly present in Hadley's design. Unfortunately, no written account was found on what Arnold may have told the meeting.

The question then becomes: why was Paul Hadley chosen by the State Flag Committee to "tweak" the Arnold and Langdon designs?

In late 1916, Hadley was a thirty-six-year-old bachelor who lived in Mooresville and took care of his widowed mother and developmentally challenged older brother. He had not yet become a gifted and well respected watercolorist. Instead, Hadley was a self-employed interior designer who apparently worked with wealthy Indianapolis clients, including two-time Pulitzer Prize fiction writer Booth Tarkington, Mrs. Carey's first cousin.[7] Tarkington may have recommended Hadley, or perhaps Mrs. Carey had availed herself of Hadley's services in the past.

In any case, the question now becomes: when was Hadley hired to work on the flag design? Based on the events described above, Hadley was likely hired sometime after the DAR convention in October 1916 when it was clear a suitable design had not yet been finalized and before January 5, 1917 when Mrs. Carey announced the design contest would remain open for another week.[8] My suspicion is that this announcement was made to allow Hadley more time to finish his design. Years later, he admitted in an interview how he had trouble finding someone to sew elements of his design together before presenting it to the legislators.[9]

Given that Hadley's design "evolved" from the designs of Arnold and Langdon, it is worth noting what he did right with his design. Hadley chose a single, blue background and kept the collection of stars in the center of his design like the Langdon flag. His single biggest change was taking the five "stray" stars shown outside the circle of stars in the Arnold and Langdon flags, and placing them in a semi-circle inside the larger circle of stars. This brought more unity to his design.

His final touch was inserting the torch in the center of the stars with six rays extending out from the flame. In an interview he did years later, Hadley said his inspiration came from the Statue of Liberty and the torch atop the Soldiers and Sailors Monument in downtown Indianapolis. He said the torch represented Liberty and Enlightenment while the rays radiating out from the torch represented the spreading of those concepts.[10] Hadley took the larger star representing Indiana and placed it above the flame while Senate Republicans added the word "Indiana" to the design.

One unresolved question I had was: who suggested the torch and radiating rays? Was it Hadley's idea or had Mrs. Carey or members of her Star Flag Committee made the suggestion. No record was found to answer that question.

Having analyzed Hadley's flag design and what appears to have transpired with it, I have no problem in declaring him the rightful designer of the state flag, although Irwin Burnett Arnold probably deserves some recognition, given how much of his flag was present in the final design.

NOTES

CHAPTER ONE: STATE FLAG INITIATIVES, 1914

1 "How The State Flag was Selected for Indiana," *The Brazil Daily Times,* 9 February 1926, p. 4. This article is a reprint of a speech given by Miss Pearl Finley to the Clay County Historical Society. It describes how the debate began on creating a unique state flag.

2 Walker, Jenny Girton, "The State Flags of Memorial Continental Hall," *D.A.R. Magazine,* Vol.. LXI, No. 2 (February 1927) pp. 100-108. The members of the State Flag Committee included: Mrs. F.F. Hutchens, Mrs. Robert McBride and Mrs. R.C. Bennett, all of Indianapolis; Mrs. Charles Thompson of Edinburgh; and Miss Ames of Greencastle. In addition to Indiana, the national DAR organization encouraged its members in Illinois, Missouri, Utah, and Wyoming to also pursue state flag laws.

3 "Daniel Stewart's Death," *Indianapolis Journal,* 25 February 1892, p. 8.

4 "John N. Carey, Civil Leader, Succumbs Here," *The Indianapolis Star,* 20 May 1938, p. 3. Also, "J.N. Carey Dead; Business Leader," *The Indianapolis News,* 19 May 1938, p. 33.

5 "Historical Sketch" in Indianapolis Woman's Club Records, 1875-2007. Contained in the Manuscripts Collections Department, William Henry Smith Memorial Library, Indiana Historical Society, 450 West Ohio Street, Indianapolis, IN.

6 For a history of the Indiana DAR, see http://www.darindiana.org/in/index.html Accessed May 11, 2020.

7 Kriplen, Nancy, *Keep An Eye On that Mummy: A History of the Children's Museum of Indianapolis,* Indianapolis: The Children's Museum of Indianapolis, 1982, <u>passim.</u>

8 "D.A.R. Shows Fine Growth," *Fort Wayne Sentinel,* 14 October, 1914, p. 1.

9 "Submits Suggested Design for an Indiana State Flag," *Fort Wayne Sentinel,* 14 October 1914, p. 1.

10 The biographical information about Irwin Burnett Arnold was gleaned from *Memoirs of Wayne County and the City of Richmond, Indiana, Vol. II,* Fox, Henry Clay editor. Madison, Wisconsin: Western Historical Association, 1912, pp. 85-89.

11 Ibid. Lessie was Arnold's third wife. The other two had died.

12 *Proceedings of Thirty-Fifth Annual Session of the Department of Indiana Grand Army of the Republic Held at Indianapolis, IND. May 6, 7, 8, 1914,* Volume XXXI, Indianapolis: Sentinel Printing Co., Printers and Binders. 1914. pp. 95-98.

13 Ibid.

14 Ibid.

15 Ibid.

16 A description of Arnold's flag is mentioned in "Indiana Is Hunting For 'Father' or 'Mother' Of Official State Flag, Has No Permanent Emblem Of Its Own To Mark Energies Of A Century," *The Indianapolis News,* 11 March 1916, p. 15. The article also has a montage of photographs of flags, including Arnold's, that was submitted for the contest.

17 "Delphi Veteran is Named Commander," *The Indianapolis News,* 8 May 1914, p. 10.

18 "Cheers For Flag End Convention," *The Indianapolis Star,* 9 May 1914, p. 3.

19 "Terre Haute Voted Next State D.A.R. Convention," *The Indianapolis Star,* 16 October 1914, p. 10.

CHAPTER TWO: THE LIBRARIAN'S FLAG, 1885

1 Several books have described the intense political partisanship that existed at the state and national levels at the end of the nineteenth century. Two books consulted on this subject were Madison, James H., *Hoosiers: A New History of Indiana.* Bloomington: University of Indiana Press, 2014 and O'Leary, Cecilia Elizabeth, *To Die For: The Paradox of American Patriotism.* Princeton: Princeton University Press, 1999.

2 Concurrent Resolution No. 6, Laws of Indiana, 1885, p. 89.

3 Gordon, John Steele, *Washington's Monument and the Fascinating History of the Obelisk.* New York: Bloomsbury, 2016.

4 See Madison and O'Leary, passim.

5 Blanchard, Charles L. Editor, *Counties of Morgan, Monroe, and Brown, Indiana Historical and Biographical.* Chicago: F. A. Battey & Co., Publisher, 1884.

6 Gugin, Linda C. and St. Clair, James E., editors, *The Governors of Indiana: A Biographical Directory.* Indianapolis: Indiana Historical Society Press, 2006.

7 "Election Results," *The Daily Evening Republic* (Columbus) 10 November 1882, p. 2.

8 "Senator Thomas J. Foster, Sends a Ball Crashing Through his Brain While Laboring Under a fit of Temporary Insanity," *Fort Wayne Daily Gazette,* 24 June 1882, p. 6.

9 *History, Art & Archives. U.S. House of Representatives,* "ENGLISH. William Eastin," https://history.house.gov/People/Listing/E/ENGLISH, -William-Eastin-(E000190)/. Accessed 29 March 2020.

10 Canup, Charles E., "The Temperance Movement in Indiana," *Indiana Magazine of History,* vol. 16, no. 2, 1920, pp. 112-151. See also Lantzer, Jason *Prohibition is Here to Stay: The Reverend Edward S. Shumaker and the Dry Crusade in Indiana.* Notre Dame, IN: University of Notre Dame Press, 2009.

11 "Fair Play," *The Huntington Democrat,* 25 January 1883, p. 2.

12 Joint Democratic Caucus, *Fort Wayne Sentinel,* 17 January 1883, p. 1.

13 See Concurrent Resolution No. 6.

14 "Afternoon Session," *The Indianapolis State Sentinel,* 3 February 1885, p. 3.

15 Bennett, Pamela J. and January, Alan "Indiana's State Seal: An Overview," Indiana Historical Bureau, 21 January 2005.

16 The description of the Callis flag is based on a visual examination of the lithograph found in Henry, William E., *The Legislative and State Manual of Indiana, 1899 and 1900,* Indianapolis: Wm. R. Burford, 1899.

17 "City News," *The Indianapolis News,* 20 February 1885, p. 3.

18 French, D.J. *The History of an Indiana Railroad: The Fairland, Franklin & Martinsville RR, 1846-1973,* self-published book, 2018, p. 16.

19 Hunt, Roger D. *Colonels in Blue — Indiana, Kentucky and Tennessee: A Civil War Biographical Dictionary.* Jefferson, NC: McFarland & Co., Inc. Publishers, 2014, p. 110. In 1849, Scott married Mary A. Gwinn.

The couple had two children, Mary Imogine and William. They all died before Scott married Callis.

20 "Mrs. Eliza O. Scott Dead," *The Daily Reporter* (Martinsville, Indiana), 21 September 1923, p. 1.

CHAPTER THREE: THE PATRIOT'S FLAG, 1901

1 *Report of the Fifteenth Annual Conference of the Indiana Chapter Daughters of the American Revolution Held in Terre Haute, Oct. 19, 20, 21, 1915,* Terre Haute, Ind.: F.J. Weldele & Co., Printers, p. 49.

2 Commemorative *biographical record of prominent and representative men of Indianapolis and vicinity, containing biographical sketches of business and professional men and of many of the early settled families,* Chicago: J.H. Beers & Co., 1908.

3 Madison, James H. Hoosiers: *A New History of Indiana.* Bloomington: Indiana University Press, 2014, pp. 151-53.

4 Dixon, Willis Milnor, *Kith and Kin: Containing Genealogical Data of the Following Families: Dixon, Andrus, Battin, Beal, Bosworth, Chapin, Converse, Capel,* Los Angeles: Hardpress Publishing, 2013. Wallace Foster's older brother, Robert Sanford Foster, became a Brigadier-General during the Civil War and one of the judges at the court martial of the individuals accused of assassinating President Abraham Lincoln.

5 Ibid.

6 Lang, Harry G. *Fighting in the Shadows: The Untold Story of Deaf People in the Civil War,* Washington, D.C.: Gallaudet University Press, 2017, pp. 219-223.

7 O'Leary, Cecilia Elizabeth. *To Die For: The Paradox of American Patriotism,* Princeton, NJ: Princeton University Press, 1999, pp. 151-55

and Leepson, Marc. *Flag: An American Biography*. New York: Thomas Dunne Books, 2005, p. 164.

8 "Wallace Foster School No. 32 Takes Pride in Having Had First Educational Flag Ceremony," *The Indianapolis News*, 12 February 1923, p. 25. See also Commemorative Biographical Record, footnote 22.

9 Balch, George T. *Methods of Teaching Patriotism in the Public Schools*. New York: D. Van Nostrand. Indianapolis: Levey Bros., 1898.

10 Foster, Wallace. *Patriotic Primer for the Little Citizen*. Hansebooks, 2017 (reprint of original).

11 Laws of Indiana, March 9, 1901, chap. 150, (SB 239) p. 336.

12 For a comprehensive look at the flag protection movement, see Goldstein, Robert Justin. *Saving "Old Glory" The History of the American Flag Desecration Controversy*. Boulder, CO: Westview Press, 1995, _passim_. See also "Statesman At Work," *The Indianapolis Journal*, 7 February 1901, p. 4, and "New Indiana Law On Desecrating Of The Flag," *The Bedford Weekly Mail,* 22 March 1901, p. 1.

13 "Outbreak of Oratory," *The Indianapolis News,* 8 March 1901, p. 2.

14 "Last Working Day," *The Muncie Daily Herald*, 9 March 1901, p. 6.

15 "The Flag," *The Columbus Republican*, 23 May 23, 1901, p. 2.

16 "The Flag," *The Richmond Palladium-Item,* 29 May 1901, p. 2.

17 "Capt. Foster, 'Flag Man,'" *The Indianapolis Star*, 1 April 1919, p. 6. Foster and his son, William, operated a flag business from his home on Capitol Avenue. William continued to run the business after his father's passing.

38 Mrs. Carey's comments, see footnote 21.

19 Ibid.

20 Ibid.

CHAPTER FOUR: THE CENTENNIAL FLAG, 1916

1 Wynn, Frank Barbour. *Suggestive Plans for a Historical and Educational Celebration in Indiana in 1916.* Indianapolis: Indiana Centennial Celebration Committee, 1912.

2 Ibid, p.16. The Museum was not built until 1902 while the Library was constructed in 1924.

3 Ibid, p. 123.

4 Woodburn, James A, "The Indiana Historical Commission and Plans for The Centennial". *Indiana Magazine of History*, Vol. 11, No. 4 (December 1915), pp. 338-347. Several other resources are available in describing the work of the Indiana Historical Commission.

5 Ibid, p. 339. Woodburn notes that lawmakers appropriated $25,000 to the Commission, of which $5,000 might be applied, if the Commission so ordered, for the publication of historical materials.

6 Ibid, p. 342. See also, McReynolds, G., "The Centennial Pageant for Indiana; Suggestions for Its Performance" *Indiana Magazine of History*, Vol. 11, No. 3 (September 1915), pp. 248-271.

7 Biographical information about William Chauncy Langdon can be found in David Glassberg's book, *American Historical Pageantry: The Uses of Tradition in the Early Twentieth Century.* Chapel Hill: The University of North Carolina Press, 1990 and from a biographical sketch of Langdon found in the William Chauncy Langdon Papers (1898-1940) at the John Hay Library, Brown University, Providence, Rhode Island.

8 See Langdon biographical sketch. Langdon's father, in addition to being an Episcopal minister, was instrumental in the establishment of the YMCA.

9 Glassberg, p. 71.

10 Ibid.

11 Harlow, Lindley, ed. *The Indiana Centennial, 1916; a Record of the Celebration of the one Hundredth Anniversary of Indiana's Admission to Statehood.* Indianapolis; The Indiana Historical Commission, 1919. p. 322.

12 Ibid., p. 322.

13 Langdon, William Chauncy, *The Pageant of Bloomington and Indiana University*, Bloomington: Indiana University Press, 1916.

14 "Bloomington Pageant," *The Fort Wayne News*, 16 May 1916, p. 11, and "Bloomington Gives Five Pageant Today," *The Indianapolis Star*, 16 May 1916, p. 4.

15 "Governor Ralston Plays In Pageant," *The Richmond Item*, 17 May 1916, p. 8.

16 "Record Crowd Sees I.U. Pageant End," *The Indianapolis News*, 18 May 1916, p. 5.

17 Langdon, William Chauncy. *The Pageant of Corydon, the Pioneer Capital of Indiana, 1816-1916; The Drama of the Preeminence of the Town at the Time When for Twelve Years It Was the Territorial and the State Capital of Indiana*, New Albany: Baker's Printing House, 1916.

18 "First State Capital Honors Centennial," *The Tribune* (Seymour), 3 June 1916, p. 3. and "Shows History of State in Pageant," *Alexandria Times-Tribune*, 2 June 1916, p. 1.

19 "Fairbanks Gives State's History," *The Indianapolis Star*, 4 June 1916, p. 3.

20 "Corydon's Celebration," *The Indianapolis Star*, 4 June 1916, p. 28.

21 Langdon, William Chauncy. *The Pageant of Indiana: The Drama of the Development of the State as a Community from its Exploration by LaSalle to the Centennial of its Admission to the Union*, Indianapolis: The Hollenbeck Press, 1916.

22 "Magnificent Costumes Enhance Beauty of Pageant Principal," The *Indianapolis Star*, 6 October 1916, p. 11. This photographic montage of several costumes worn at the Pageant of Indiana showed Langdon's daughter, Elizabeth, holding her father's flag, but it was not unfurled and therefore its full design could not be seen.

23 "Indiana University Celebrates 100th Anniversary Today," *The Richmond Palladium-Item*, 20 January 1920, p. 12 and "I.U. Reunion Will be held from May 30 to June 4th," *The Richmond Palladium-Item*, 17 May 1920, p. 7.

24 Langdon biographical sketch.

25 "Other Centennial Celebrations," https://www.in.gov/library/about/general-information/exhibits/centennial-indiana/ Accessed March 16, 2022.

26 Langdon letter to Gov. Ralston, May 23, 1916. Accessed from Indiana State Archives. See also *Report of the Fifteenth Annual Conference of the Indiana Chapter Daughters of the American Revolution Held in Terre Haute, Oct. 19, 20, 21, 1915*. Terre Haute, Ind.: F.J. Weldele & Co., Printers, p. 49.

27 Ibid.

28 See reference to the flag photograph at footnote 22.

29 "Indiana Is Hunting For 'Father' or "Mother' Of Official State Flag, Has No Permanent Emblem Of Its Own To Mark Energies Of A Century," *The Indianapolis News*, 11 March 1916, p. 15.

30 Ibid.

31 Report *of the Sixteenth Annual Conference of the Indiana Chapter, Daughters of the American Revolution, held in Richmond, Oct. 24, 25, 26, 1916*, (no publication credit given) pp. 68-69.

32 Ibid.

33 Ibid.

CHAPTER FIVE: ENACTING A STATE BANNER, 1917

1 "Still Time For Some One to Submit New Ideas in State Flag Contest," *The Indianapolis News,* 5 January 1917, p. 3.

2 Hill, Herbert R., "The Indiana State Flag and Seal — Symbols of Hoosier Independence," *Outdoor Indiana*, Vol. 40, No. 7, September 1975, pp. 23-29.

3 See footnote 1.

4 Ibid.

5 Ibid.

6 Laws of Indiana, Chap. 164, (SB 344) p. 346. 1917.

7 Ibid.

8 Ibid.

9 Finch, Evan, "Birth of a Banner: The Origins of Indiana's State Flag," *Commercial Magazine* 10 (2017), pp. 26-35.

10 "Indiana Ranks Third In Recruits," *Bloomington Evening World*, 20 April 1917, p. 1.

11 "Indiana's Surpassing Record," *The Hancock Democrat*, 17 May 1917, p. 5.

12 "The United State World War I Centennial Committee" https://www.worldwar1centennial.org/index.php/indiana-wwi-centennial-home.html. Accessed 12 May 2020.

13 "Indianapolis Men Wire For Peace, *The Indianapolis Star*, 4 April 1017, p. 9.

14 "Indiana D.A.R. Are Asked To Join And Assist The Red Cross," *The Indianapolis News*, 7 February 1917, p. 3.

15 "Artists' Posters Feature of Military Garden Party," *The Indianapolis News*, 21 June 1917, p. 7.

16 "Hoosiers Who Do Things," *The Indianapolis Star*, 12 July 1942, p. 5.

17 "Indiana State Banner Displayed By D.A.R." The *Indianapolis News*, 8 November 1917, p. 13. The Indiana D.A.R. contingent presented a state banner to its national organization in 1919. See "Shows Work of Indiana D.A.R.," *The Indianapolis Star*, 18 April 1919, p. 5.

18 "Flag for Battleship," The *Indianapolis News*, 17 December 1917, p. 11.

19 "Captain of Battleship Indiana Writes Letter, The *Indianapolis News*, 19 January 1918, p. 14.

20 "Indiana Day Adds Interest in Original State Banner Model," The *Indianapolis News*, 11 December 1931, p. 20.

CHAPTER SIX: THE BANNER YEARS, 1917-1955

1 "The Indiana Flag," *The Indianapolis Star,* 7 October 1920, p. 6. See also "The Indiana Banner," *The Indianapolis News,* 26 November 1920, p. 6.

2 Ibid.

3 "Built 91 Years Ago," *The Indianapolis News,* 17 September 1923, p. 16.

4 "Notes of the State D.A.R.," *The Indianapolis News,* 10 November 1923, p. 23.

5 "Flag of Indiana Gets Place in Court of P.O. Department," *The Indianapolis News,* 6 June 1923, p. 20.

6 "State Banner Bows To 'Old Glory' On Capitol," *The Indianapolis Star,* 4 March 1923, p. 9.

7 "Indiana State Flag Prints Are Being Distributed To Children," *The Indianapolis News,* 10 December 1925, p. 25.

8 "Schools Receive Indiana Banners As Local Gifts," *Journal and Courier* (Lafayette, Indiana), 29 May 1928, p. 12 and "Activities of Indiana D.A.R.," *The Indianapolis Star,* 3 June 1928, p. 30..

9 "The Orchard School" www.orchard.org. Accessed 13 May 2020.

10 Kriplen, Nancy, *Keep An Eye On That Mummy: A History of the Children's Museum of Indianapolis,* Indianapolis: The Children's Museum of Indianapolis, 1982. Mrs. Carey donated her Meridian Street home to the Museum after buying a country estate on the city's northwest side. Her new place was known as Haverway Farm. See Freeland, Sharon Butsch, "Haverway Farm," Historical Indianapolis.com, Sept.

2, 2014. https://historicindianapolis.com/hi-mailbag-haverway-farm/ Accessed 7 June 2021.

11 Ibid.

12 "Mrs. John Newman Carey, Civic and Social Club Leader, Dies," *The Indianapolis News*, 15 June 1938, p. 1 and "Mrs. John N. Carey, Art Patron, Dies; Led Movement to Adopt State Flag," *The Indianapolis Star*, 15 June 1938, p. 1.

13 "The Market Street Art Gallery," https://weeklyview.net/2019/02/21/the-market-street-art-colony/. Accessed 4 April 2020.

14 "Water Colors by Hadley," *The Indianapolis Star*, 4 December 1921, p. 64.

15 Biographical information about Paul Hadley can be found at, Rebecca Hardin, *The Indiana State flag, its designer: biography of Paul Hadley with anthology of his paintings.* Mooresville, IN: Self-published, 1976 and Rachel B. Perry, "Paul Hadley: Artist and designer of the Indiana Flag," *Traces of Indiana and Midwestern History*, 15 (1), (2003), pp. 20-29.

16 The Indiana Historical Bureau photograph of Paul Hadley watching Herron student Ralph E. Priest applying gold leaf to an Indiana state flag can be viewed with Perry's magazine article on Hadley.

17 See Perry's magazine article, footnote 15.

18 "Donald M. Mattison Herron Art Director," *The Indianapolis News*, 13 May 1933, p. 10. See also Warkel, Harriet G., Krause, Martin F. and Berry, S.L. The Herron Chronicle, Bloomington: Indiana University Press, 2003.

19 See Perry's magazine article on Paul Hadley. After the Progress Exhibition, the Benton murals were stored at the Indiana State Fair-

grounds in Indianapolis until Indiana University President Herman B. Wells had them sent to the University and put on display. It is not known if Hadley's benches were part of that transfer or it they ended up somewhere else.

20 "The History Museum," https://historymuseumsb.org/ Accessed 12 November 2020.

21 "Machinist's Plea Results In Indiana Flag for Hawaii," *The South Bend Tribune*, 7 December 1942, p. 11. See also, "Henry F. Schricker" in *The Governors of Indiana*, pp. 308-315.

22 "Paul Hadley's Landscapes Are Finest Type of Realism," *The Indianapolis Star*, 7 September 1947, p. 70.

23 "State Flag Soon to Hang in Japan," The *Indianapolis News*, 30 July 1951, p. 15.

24 "Indiana's Flag Flies In Korea," The *Indianapolis Star*, 23 November 1951, p. 10. See also "Bedford Soldier In Korea Wants An Indiana Flag," The *Bedford Daily-Times Mail*, 5 July 1951, p.1.

25 "Indiana Banner Now Is in Thick of Fight," The *Indianapolis News*, 16 September 1952, p. 17.

26 "The Things I hear!" *The Indianapolis Star*, 16 September 1947, p. 17.

CHAPTER SEVEN: HADLEY'S STATE FLAG, 1955-2016

1 "Star Flag Urged," *The Indianapolis Star*, 12 January 1955, p. 3.

2 "Bury Last Indiana Civil War Veteran," *Logansport Pharos-Tribune*, 21 February 1949, p. 2.

3 "George N. Craig," in *The Governors of Indiana*, pp. 322-329.

4 Laws of Indiana, (SB 47) 1955. The lone Senate dissenter was Thomas C. Hasbrook of Indianapolis. See "Thomas C. Hasbrook, 75, dies: had been deputy mayor, lawmaker," *The Indianapolis Star*, 6 October 1995, p. 80 and "Success Story U.S. Style: Tom Hasbrook," *The Noblesville Ledger*, 11 July 1969, p. 8.

5 See SB 47.

6 "Three resolutions passed by Indiana state senate Wednesday," *The Kokomo Morning Times*, 25 February 1965, p. 5.

7 "Legislative Calendar," *The Indianapolis Star*, 3 March 1965, p. 15.

8 "Indiana Stamp Ceremony Set," *The South Bend Tribune*, 15 April 1966, p. 26.

9 "Branigin Unveils Sesquicentennial Postage Stamp," *The Herald (Jasper)*, 16 April 1966, p. 1.

10 "City Artist Wins Sesquicentennial Design Contest," *The Indianapolis News*, 19 November 1964, p. 31.

11 "Corydon PO to Inaugurate State Sesqui Stamp Sales, *The Terre Haute Star*, 16 April 1966, p. 6.

12 See advertisement for sale of small Indiana State Flags in *The Bedford Daily Times-Mail*, 23 June 1962, p. 3.

13 "Fly a Flag Feb 12, Lincoln's Birthday," Advertisement found in *The Star-Press* (Muncie), 3 February 1967, p. 17.

14 "Bicentennial Commission Members Appointed By Gov. Whitcomb," *The Kokomo Tribune*, 24 November 1971, p. 4.

15 "Helmke To Head Bicentennial Unit," *The Indianapolis Star*, 10 May 1975, p. 19.

16 "The Hoosier Day," *Rushville Republican*, 8 September 1975, p. 4.

17 "Clark Trail Is Dedicated," *The Vincennes Sun-Commercial*, 20 November 1975, p. 1.

18 "Book Tells History of Effort in West," *The Muncie Star*, 25 July 1976, Sec. B. p. 7.

19 See advertisement "State of Indiana American Revolution Bicentennial Medal," *The Times (Munster)*, 5 October 1973, p. 7.

20 "Bicentennial unit looking for leader," *Journal and Courier (Lafayette)*, 26 June 1976, p. 15.

21 "Statehouse Ceremony Among Events Scheduled For July 4 Holiday Weekend," *Palladium-Item (Richmond)*, 1 July 1976, p. 18. See also "Pyle Home Becomes Memorial," *The Indianapolis News*, 5 July 1976, p. 10.

22 Ibid.

23 "About Stamps and Coins," *The Cincinnati Enquirer*, 24 August 1975, p. 11-B.

24 "Indiana recognized," *The Daily Journal (Franklin)*, 13 July 1976, p. 12.

25 "Commission Will Hold Closing Ceremonies," *Vidette-Messenger of Porter County (Valparaiso, IN)*, 18 December 1976, p. 2.

26 "Indiana Bicentennial Celebrations 2016" https://www.in.gov/ibc. Accessed 14 May 2020.

27 "Bicentennial Kick-off," https://www.in.gov/ibc/4522.htm. Accessed 14 May 2020.

28 "Bicentennial Legacy Projects," https://www.in.gov/ibc/2351.htm. Accessed 14 May 2020.

29 "Torch Relay," https://www.in.gov/ibc/torchrelay/index.htm. Accessed 14 May 2020.

CHAPTER EIGHT: MOORESVILLE'S LOVE AFFAIR
WITH PAUL HADLEY

1 Newton, Judith Vale, Gerdts, William H. *Hoosier Group: Five American Painters*, Indianapolis: Eckert Publications, 1985.

2 "Rachel B. Perry, "Paul Hadley: Artist and designer of the Indiana Flag," *Traces of Indiana and Midwestern History*, 15 (1), (2003), pp. 20-29.

3 "Dr. Evan Hadley Dead," *The Indianapolis Journal*, 13 May 1903, p. 7.

4 See Perry article, passim.

5 Ibid.

6 "Notes of Interest in Life of Paul Hadley, Designer of the Indiana State Flag," These facts were gleaned from relatives and close friends by the Mooresville Public Library.

7 See Perry article, passim.

8 "Becky Shields Romine Hardin," *The Indianapolis Star*, 22 July 1995, p. 50. Also, "A Bit of Becky Hardin..." *The Reporter-Times (Martinsville)*, 26 July 1995, p. 3.

9 Ibid.

10 "Home-of-State-Flag Slogan Adopted," *The Indianapolis Star*, 10 November 1966, p. 27 and "Mooresville Plays Up State Flag Connection," *The Reporter-Times (Martinsville)*, 11 November 1966, p. 1.

11 "Large Crowd Attends Junior High Dedication," *The Reporter-Times (Martinsville)*, 28 March 1966, p. 1.

12 Perry article, passim.

13 "Designer Of State Flag Dies; Came Here in 1967," *The Richmond Palladium-Item*, 1 February 1971, p. 9 and "Paul Hadley, Designer Of Indiana Flag, Dies," *The Indianapolis Star*, 2 February 1971, p. 25.

14 A copy of the Senate resolution upon Hadley's death is available at the Mooresville Public Library.

15 Rebecca Hardin, *The Indiana State flag, its designer: biography of Paul Hadley with anthology of his paintings*, (Self-published book, 1976).

16 "Spunky Woman," *Rushville Republican*, 28 September 1976, p. 4.

17 "A Bit of Becky Hardin..." *The Daily Reporter* (Martinsville), 26 July 1995, p. 3.

18 For a summary of Bicentennial Events in Morgan County, see: https://www.in.gov/ibc/2418.htm Accessed 14 May 2020.

19 For a summary of the Legacy Projects of the Mooresville Redevelopment Commission, see: https://www.in.gov/ibc/legacyprojects/3063.htm and https://www.in.gov/ibc/legacyprojects/3056.htm.

20 "Projects raising questions, concerns: Town's redevelopment commission at issue," *The Reporter-Times (Martinsville)*, 30 December 2017 and "Projects put spotlight on redevelopment, TIFs," *The Reporter-Times (Martinsville)*, 3 January 2018.

21 See information on the various Morgan County Legacy Projects events at: https://www.in.gov/ibc/2418.htm Accessed 14 May 2020. See also "Paul Hadley's template of the state flag," *The Reporter-Times (Martinsville)*, 6 May 2000.

22 "Flagpole, plaque honoring Hadley dedicated," *The Reporter-Times (Martinsville)*, 29 June 2016.

23 "Paul Hadley flag marker dedicated," *The Reporter-Times (Martinsville)*, 13 August 2016.

24 Ibid.

CHAPTER NINE: WHO REALLY DESIGNED THE STATE FLAG?

1 *Report of the Fifteenth Annual Conference of the Indiana Chapter, Daughters of the American Revolution Held in Terre Haute, Oct. 19, 20, 21, 1915*, Terre Haute, Ind., F.J. Weldele & Co., Printers, p. 49.

2 "Indiana Is Hunting For 'Father' or 'Mother' Of Official State Flag, Has No Permanent Emblem Of Its Own To Mark Energies Of A Century," *The Indianapolis News*, 11 March 1916, p. 15.

3 *Report of the Sixteenth Annual Conference of the Indiana Chapter, Daughters of the American Revolution held in Richmond, Oct. 24, 25, 26, 1916*, (no publication credit given), pp. 68-69.

4 "Still Time For Some One to Submit New Ideas in State Flag Contest," *The Indianapolis News*, 5 January 1917, p. 3.

5 Hill, Herbert R., "The Indiana State Flag and Seal — Symbols of Hoosier Independence," *Outdoor Indiana*, Vol. 40, No. 7, September 1975, pp. 23-29.

6 See footnote 3 for a brief mention of the discussion among the design experts.

7 See Perry, Rachel B., "Paul Hadley: Artist and designer of the Indiana Flag," *Traces of Indiana and Midwestern History,* 15 (1) (2003), pp. 20-29.

8 Ibid.

9 Ibid.

10 Ibid.

SELECT BIBLIOGRAPHY

BOOKS

Balch, George T. *Methods of Teaching Patriotism in the Public Schools.* New York: D. van Nostrand. Indianapolis: Levey Bros, 1898.

Barnhart, John D. *Indiana The Hoosier State.* New York: Harper & Row, 1959.

Blanchard, Charles L. Editor, *Counties of Morgan, Monroe, and Brown, Indiana Historical and Biographical.* Chicago: F. A. Battey & Co., Publisher. 1884.

Boomhower, Ray E. *To Be Hoosiers: Historic Stories of Character & Fortitude.* Charleston, SC: The History Press, 2020.

Commemorative biographical record of prominent and representative men of Indianapolis and vicinity containing biographical sketches of business and professional men and of many of the early settled families. Chicago: J.H. Beers & Co., 1908.

Derzipilski, Kathleen, Hantula, Richard and Bjorklund, Ruth. *Indiana; the Hoosier State.* New York: Cavendish Square, 2017.

Dixon, Willis Milnor. *Kith and Kin: Containing Genealogical Data of the Following Families: Dixon, Andrus, Battin, Beal, Bosworth, Chapin, Converse, Copel.* Los Angeles: Hardpress Publishing, 2013. (reprint of original).

Foster, Wallace. *The deaf soldier: a brief synopsis of one hundred and two cases of deafness, prepared for the consideration of the Senate and House of Representatives of the United States.* Nabu Press, 2010. (reprint of original).

_____. *Patriotic Primer for the Little Citizen*. Hansebooks, 2017. (reprint of original).

Fox, Henry Clay, editor, *Memoirs of Wayne County and the City of Richmond, Indiana, Vol. II,*

Madison, WI: Western Historical Association, 1912.

French, D.J. *The History of an Indiana Railroad: The Fairland, Franklin & Martinsville RR. 1846-1973*. Martinsville, IN.: Self-published book, 2018.

Glassberg, David. *American Historical Pageantry: The Uses of Tradition in the Early Twentieth Century*. Chapel Hill: The University of North Carolina Press, 1990.

Goldstein, Robert Justin. *Saving "Old Glory" The History of the American Flag Controversy*. Boulder, CO; Westview Press, 1995.

Gordon John Steele. *Washington's Monument and the Fascinating History of the Obelisk*. New York: Bloomsbury USA 2006.

Gray, R.D. *The Hoosier State: Readings in Indiana History (v.1)*. Bloomington: Indiana University Press, 1982.

_____*Indiana History: A Book of Readings*. Bloomington: Indiana University Press, 1994.

Gugin, Linda C. and St. Clair, James E., editors, *The Governors of Indiana: A Biographical Directory*. Indianapolis: Indiana Historical Society Press, 2006.

Hardin, Becky. *The Indiana State flag, its designer: biography of Paul Hadley with anthology of his paintings*. Mooresville, IN: Self-published, 1976.

Harlow, Lindley, ed. *The Indiana Centennial, 1916; a Record of the Celebration of the one Hundredth Anniversary of Indiana's Admission to Statehood.* Indianapolis: The Indiana Historical Commission, 1919.

Hendrickson, Walter B. *The Indiana Years 1903-1941.* Indianapolis: Indiana Historical Society. 1983.

Henry, William E. *The Legislative and State Manual of Indiana, 1899 and 1900.* Indianapolis: Wm. R. Burford, 1899.

Howe, Randy. *Flags of the Fifty States,* Second Edition. Guilford, Connecticut: The Lyons Press, 2010.

Hunt, Roger D. *Colonels in Blue — Indiana, Kentucky and Tennessee: A Civil War Biographical Dictionary.* Jefferson, N.C.: McFarland & Co., Inc. Publishers, 2014.

Kriplen, Nancy. *Keep An Eye On That Mummy: A History of The Children's Museum of Indianapolis.* Indianapolis: The Children's Museum of Indianapolis, 1982.

Lang, Harry G. *Fighting in the Shadows: The Untold Story of Deaf People in the Civil War.* Washington, D.C.: Gallaudet University Press, 1992.

Langdon, William Chauncy. *The Pageant of Bloomington and Indiana University.* Bloomington: Indiana University Press, 1916.

_____. *The Pageant of Corydon, the Pioneer Capital of Indiana, 1816-1916: The Drama of the Preeminence of the Town at the Time When for Twelve Years It Was the Territorial and the State Capital of Indiana.* New Albany: Baker's Printing House, 1916.

_____. *The Pageant of Indiana: The Drama of the Development of the State as a Community from its Exploration by LaSalle to the Centennial of its Admission to the Union.* Indianapolis: The Hollenbeck Press, 1916.

_____. *Everyday things in American life, 1776-1876.* New York: Scribner, 1941.

Lantzer, Jason. *Prohibition is Here to Stay: The Reverend Edward S. Shumaker and the Dry Crusade in Indiana.* Notre Dame, IN: University of Notre Dame Press, 2009.

Leepson, Marc. *Flag: An American Biography.* New York: Thomas Dunne Books, 2005.

Madison, James H. *Hoosiers: A New History of Indiana.* Bloomington: University of Indiana Press, 2014.

McConnell, Stuart. *Glorious Contentment: The Grand Army of the Republic, 1865-1900.* Chapel Hill: The University of North Carolina Press, 1992.

Morgan, Francesca. *Women and Patriotism in Jim Crow America.* Chapel Hill: University of North Carolina Press, 2005.

Newton, Judith Vale, Gerdts, William H., *Hoosier Group: Five American Painters,* Indianapolis: Eckert Publications, 1985.

O'Leary, Cecilia Elizabeth, *To Die For: The Paradox of American Patriotism.* Princeton: Princeton University Press, 1999.

Phillips, Clifton J. *Indiana in Transition: The Emergence of an Industrial Commonwealth, 1880-1920.* Indianapolis: Indiana Historical Bureau and Indiana Historical Society, 1968.

Proceedings of Thirty-Fifth Annual Session of the Department of Indiana Grand Army of the Republic Held at Indianapolis, Ind, May 6, 7, 8, 1914, Volume XXXI, Indianapolis: Sentinel Printing Co., Printers and Binders, 1914, pp. 95-98.

Report of the Fifteenth Annual Conference of the Indiana Chapter, Daughters of the American Revolution Held in Terre Haute, Oct. 19, 20,21, 1915. Terre Haute, Ind.: F.J. Weldele & Co., Printers, p. 49.

Report of the Sixteenth Annual Conference of the Indiana Chapter, Daughters of the American Revolution, held in Richmond, Oct. 24, 25, 26, 1916 (no publication credit given), pp. 68-69.

Schouten, Rudy. *The Historic Memorial District of Downtown Indianapolis,* Charleston, SC: The History Press, 2020.

Smith, Whitney. *The Flag Book of the United States,* 2nd edition, New York: William Morrow & Company, 1975.

Warkel, Harriet C., Krause, Martin F., and Berry, S.L. *The Herron Chronicle,* Indianapolis: Indiana University Press, 2003.

Wynn, Frank Barbour. *Suggestive Plans for a Historical and Educational Celebration in Indiana in 1916.* Indianapolis: Indiana Centennial Celebration Committee, 1912.

JOURNAL ARTICLES

Barrett, E., D. Brown, C. Coleman, J. Dunn, and C. Moores. "The Indiana Centennial Library and Museum Building: Two Documents," *Indiana Magazine of History,* Mar. 1911,

Boomhower, Ray E. "Celebrating Indiana's 1916 Centennial". *Traces of Indiana and Midwestern History,* Vol. 3, No. 3 (Summer 1991), p. 28,

Canup, Charles E. "The Temperance Movement in Indiana," *Indiana Magazine of History,* vol. 16, no. 2, 1920, pp. 112-151.

"Donald Carmony — Mr. Indiana History," *Indiana Magazine of History,* Vol. 72, No. 3, September 1976.

Hill, Herbert R. "The Indiana State Flag and Seal — Symbols of Hoosier Independence," *Outdoor Indiana,* Vol. 40, No. 7, September 1975, pp. 23-29.

Hoy Suellen. "Governor Samuel M. Ralston and Indiana's Centennial Celebration." *Indiana Magazine of History,* Sept. 1975, pp. 245-68.

Finch, Evan. "Birth of a Banner: The Origins of Indiana's State Flag," *Commercial Magazine* 10 (2017), pp. 26-35.

Madison, J. "Civil War Memories and "Pardnership Forgittin,"" 1865–1913". *Indiana Magazine of History,* Sept. 2003,

McReynolds, G. "The Centennial Pageant for Indiana; Suggestions for Its Performance." *Indiana Magazine of History,* Sept. 1915,

Perry, Rachel B. "Paul Hadley: Artist and designer of the Indiana Flag," *Traces of Indiana and Midwestern History,* 15 (1), (2003), pp. 20-29.

Walker, Jenny Girton. "The State Flags of Memorial Continental Hall," *D.A.R. Magazine,* Vol. LXI, No. 2 (February 1927), pp. 100-108.

Woodburn, James. "The Indiana Historical Commission and Plans for The Centennial." *Indiana Magazine of History,* Dec. 191

WEBSITES CONSULTED

Bennett, Pamela J. and January, Alan, "Indiana's State Seal: An Overview," *Indiana Historical Bureau.* www.in.gov/history/2804.htm. Accessed 30 March 2020.

"Bicentennial Kick-off," https://www.in.gov/ibc/4522.htm. Accessed 14 May 2020.

"Bicentennial Legacy Projects," https://www.in.gov/ibc/2351.htm. Accessed 14 May 2020.

"Captain and Brevet Lieutenant Colonel George T. Balch," www.goordnance.army.mil/hof/2000/2001/balch.html. Accessed 9 May 2020.

"The Children's Museum of Indianapolis," https://www.childrensmuseum.org/. Accessed 13 May 2020.

"DAR History," https://www.dar.org/national-society/about-dar/dar-history. Accessed 11 May 2020.

"History of the Indiana DAR," https://www.darindiana.org/in/. Accessed 11 May 2020.

See Freeland, Sharon Butsch, "Haverway Farm," *Historical Indianapolis.com*, Sept. 2, 2014. https://historicindianapolis.com/hi-mailbag-haverway-farm/ Accessed June 7, 2021.

"The History Museum," https://historymuseumsb.org/ Accessed 12 November 2020.

"Indiana Bicentennial Celebrations 2016," https://www.in.gov/ibc/. Accessed 14 May 2020.

"The Market Street Art Gallery," https://weeklyview.net/2019/02/21/the-market-street-art-colony/. Accessed 4 April 2020.

"Mooresville SR 67 & Indiana Street Obelisk Gateway, https://www.in.gov/ibc/legacyprojects/3063.htm and "Mooresville Paul Hadley Bicentennial Park," https://www.in.gov/ibc/legacyprojects/3056.htm. Accessed 14 May 2020.

"Morgan County," https://www.in.gov/ibc/2418.htm. Accessed 14 May 2020.

"Morgan County Q&A with County Coordinator David Reddick, https://www.in.gov/ibc/2418.htm. Accessed 14 May 2020.

"The Orchard School" www.orchard.org. Accessed 13 May 2020.

"Other Centennial Celebrations," https://www.in.gov/library/2522.htm. Accessed 11 May 2020

"Torch Relay," https://www.in.gov/ibc/torchrelay/index.htm. Accessed May 14, 2020.

"U.S. Population, 1790-2000: Always Growing," www.U-S-history.com /pages/h980.html Accessed 6 April 2020.

"The United State World War I Centennial Committee" https://www.worldwar1centennial.org/index.php/indiana-wwi-centennial-home.html. Accessed 12 May 2020.

MANUSCRIPT COLLECTIONS

"Biographical Sketch," of William Chauncy Langdon found in the William Chauncy Langdon Papers (1898-1940) at the John Hay Library, Brown University, Providence, Rhode Island.

"Historical Sketch" in Indianapolis Woman's Club Records, 1875-2007. Contained in the Manuscript Collections Department, William Henry Smith Memorial Library, Indiana Historical Society, 450 West Ohio Street, Indianapolis, IN.

NEWSPAPERS

The Bedford Daily Times-Mail (1942-1972)
The Bedford Weekly Mail (1898-1919)
Bloomington Evening World (1901-1917)

Brazil Daily Times (1907-1958)

The Cincinnati Enquirer (1841-present)

The Columbus Republican (1872-1974)

The Daily Evening Republic (Columbus) (1877-1967)

The Daily Journal (Franklin) (1963-present)

The Daily Reporter (Martinsville) (1889-1946)

Fort Wayne Daily Gazette (1864-1899)

The Fort Wayne News (1884-1923)

Fort Wayne Sentinel (1870-1923)

The Hancock Democrat (1860-1957)

The Herald (Jasper) (1895-present)

The Huntington Democrat (1861-1897)

The Indiana State Sentinel (1841-1852)

The Indianapolis Journal (1887-1904)

The Indianapolis News (1869-1902; 1917-1920)

The Indianapolis Sentinel (1885)

The Indianapolis Star (1903-present)

Journal and Courier (Lafayette) (1920-present)

The Kokomo Morning Times (1964-1967)

The Kokomo Tribune (1868-1999)

The Logansport Pharos-Tribune (1890-2006)

Morgan County Democrat (1875-1970)

Morgan County Gazette (1855-1875)

The Muncie Daily Herald (1892-1906)

The Muncie Daily Star (1899-present)

The Muncie Star-Press (1900-present)

The Noblesville Ledger (1869-2008)

The Reporter-Times (Martinsville) (1892-present)

The Richmond Item (1877-1939)

The Richmond Palladium-Item (1877- present)

Rushville Republican (1889-1977)

The South Bend Tribune (1873-2019)

The Star Press (Muncie) (1900-present)

The Terre Haute Star (1861-1973)

The Times (Munster) (1906-present)

The Tribune (Seymour) (1896-present)

The Vidette-Messenger of Porter County (Valparaiso)
    (1927-1989)

The Vincennes Sun-Commercial (1804- present)

PHOTO CREDITS

Page 1 – The Children's Museum of Indianapolis Collection, 1930s.

Page 4 – *The Indianapolis Star,* May 1914.

Page 4 – Advertisement, Champaign (Ill.) *Daily Gazette,* November 1885.

Page 11 – Indiana Public Library, 1883.

Page 12 – *Encyclopedia of Biography of Indiana,* Volume 2, 1899.

Page 14 – National Park Service, February 1885.

Page 15 – Legislative and State Manual of Indiana, 1903.

Page 17 – Craig Dunn Photo Collection, 1861-1865.

Page 19 – *The Indianapolis News,* June 1916.

Page 20 – U.S. Army Ordnance School, 1863.

Page 21 – *Legare Street Press,* 2022 (reprint).

Page 22 – 45-star U.S. Flag, 1901.

Page 23 – Jeff R. Bridgeman American Antiques, 2021.

Page 28 – American Historical Pageantry, 1990.

Page 31 – National Photo Company Collection, 1923.

Page 34 – *The Indianapolis Star,* September 1916.

Page 35 – *The Indianapolis News,* March 1916.

Page 37 – Mooresville Public Library, 2001.

Page 43 – U.S. Navy, 1895.

Page 47 –The Children's Museum of Indianapolis, 1930s.

Page 48 – Bass Photo Co. Collection, Indiana Historical Society, 1014.

Page 49 – Mooresville Public Library, 2021.

Page 56 – U.S. Postal Service, 1966.

Page 57 – *Bedford Daily Times-Mail,* June 23, 1962.

Page 59 – U.S. Postal Service, 1976.

Page 60 – Indiana Bicentennial Commission, 2016.

Page 61 – Indiana Bicentennial Commission, 2016.

Page 65 – Martinsville Reporter-Times, July, 1995.

Page 68 – Rundell, Ernstberger Associates, 2016.

Page 69 – Rundell, Ernstberger Associates, 2016.

Page 73 – Mooresville Public Library, 2003.

ACKNOWLEDGEMENTS

Librarians don't know everything.
They just know how to find out everything.

Truer words were never spoken. Unfortunately, I don't know who is responsible for this quote (I was too embarrassed to ask a librarian), but I can attest that without the help of certain librarians, this book would not have been possible and especially in the middle of the COVID-19 pandemic.

First, special thanks to two "local" librarians. Janice Kistler, the reference and genealogy librarian at the Morgan County Public Library in Martinsville. She tracked down information on Eliza "Lizzie" Callis, the state librarian who designed the state's first flag. William Buckley, the recently retired information director at the Mooresville Public Library in Mooresville, answered multiple questions about Paul Hadley and shared a previously unpublished photograph of him.

Richard DeTorre and Max Perkins of the Indianapolis Public Library chased down some questions about Captain Wallace

Foster and "Old Glory" while Tamara Hemmerlein, director of local history services and Matt Holdzkom, collections assistant at the Indiana Historical Society both looked up information on William Chauncy Langdon and any photographs of his Centennial flag.

Andrea Glenn, state documents coordinator at the Indiana State Library answered numerous questions during the pandemic on different aspects of my research. She was always prompt with her email responses. Sarah Pfundstein helped track down DAR documents for me.

Likewise, two librarians at the John Hay Library at Brown University in Providence, Rhode Island, Jennifer Betts and Holly Snyder, provided biographical information on William Chauncy Langdon and a list of correspondence he had with Hoosiers during the state's Centennial celebration.

Two Morgan County residents, Mark Lemieux, senior vice-president and chief experience officer for Citizens Bank in Mooresville and Janice Bolinger, a former honorary state regent with the Indiana Daughters of the American Revolution, helped secure the funding in 2016 for the state flag historical marker in downtown Mooresville. I was the Morgan County coordinator for the state Bicentennial at the time.

Evan Finch, who I "discovered" while doing research about the state flag on *Newspapers.com* freely shared what information he already had found on the flag and gave me a copy of the article he wrote. He's a terrific researcher.

Finally, I am indebted to Candice A. Cooper who spent hours doing different graphics projects to make this book possible. Patty Dow did a wonderful job of editing the manuscript. And, my colleagues at the Greater Greenwood Toastmasters club were very patient in listening to me "test" certain aspects of the book on them.

I am also deeply indebted to Robin Surface, president of Fideli Publishing, Inc. for her tireless work in helping me put this manuscript together for publication.

Any errors in the text are not the fault of any of these individuals but are mine alone.

THE STATE FLAG
HISTORICAL MARKER

Location: Intersection of E. Main Street and Indiana Street, Mooresville (Morgan County, Indiana)

Installed 2016 Indiana Historical Bureau, Indiana Daughters of the American Revolution, Celebrate Mooresville, and Citizens Bank

ID#: 55.2016.1

Visit the *Indiana History Blog* to learn more about Paul Hadley and the Indiana State Flag.

Text on the markers

Side One

At centennial of statehood in 1916, Indiana lacked a unique state flag. The Indiana DAR spearheaded a movement to create a design by hosting a state competition. Mooresville watercolorist and John Herron Art Institute instructor Paul Hadley submitted the winning design.

Side Two

Indiana General Assembly adopted Hadley's design in 1917, but it was not widely recognized by the public. Soldiers serving in WWII, Korean, and Vietnam requested flags as a symbol of home. Celebration of Indiana's sesquicentennial in 1966 further established Hadley's design as the official state flag and successfully encouraged its wider use and recognition.

DOES THE STATE FLAG
NEED A FACELIFT?

In 2001, the North American Vexillological Association (NAVA), an organization dedicated to the study and design of flags, held a contest among its members and the public to select the best and worse flags in North America.

Seventy-two flags representing the 50 state and U.S. territorial flags as well as 13 Canadian provincial and territorial flags were part of the contest. More than 100 NAVA members and 300 members of the public representing 20 different countries judged the flags.

The top three finishers were the states of New Mexico and Texas as well as the province of Quebec. Each flag received an average score of more than eight points on a ten-point scale. The lowest-rated flag was the state of Georgia with a score of 2.36 because of the use of its state seal, lettering and a series of historical miniature state flags.

Indiana's state flag ranked 32nd with a 5.77 score.

NAVA member Edward B. Kaye wrote a booklet about the contest entitled *"Good Flag, Bad Flags and the Great Nava Flag Survey of 2001."* In it, Kaye outlined five principles of good flag design. They included:

- Keep It Simple (so even a child can understand the design);

- Use Meaningful Symbolism;

- Use 2-3 Basic Colors;

- ^a No Lettering or Seals; and

- Be Distinctive or Be Related.

Since 2001, others — mostly writers of internet blogs -- have conducted similar contests. Indiana has fared better, being named 23rd in one contest and 15th in another.

Ranking state flags can be contagious and it caused me to want to rank and tweak Paul Hadley's design. Below, is the result of my own effort. It is based on NAVA's five principles and my own ideas for a flag facelift.

The Indiana flag deserves positive marks for its relatively simple design, meaningful symbolism, 2 or 3 basic colors, and for being distinctive for having a torch as part of its design. Obviously, it falls short for violating NAVA's principle for having the state's name scrolled across the top.

What would I do to give the flag a facelift?

First, remove the state's name. This is what happens when politicians are allowed to become flag designers. Second, take the five "stray" stars and incorporate them into the circle of the thirteen original stars.

The new Mississippi flag (they were the 20th state admitted to the Union) incorporates all the stars into a single circle. The result is very attractive in my opinion. Next, leave a space between the top of the flame and the circle of stars for the larger star representing Indiana. This will draw more attention to the larger star.

Finally, remove the rays emanating from the torch. Hadley once complained that folks who made copies of his flag often faced the two bottom rays downward instead of upward.

Let me know what you think. Email your comments to
dreddick1947@gmail.com

ABOUT THE AUTHOR

David B. Reddick, a native of Canada, spent the first 20 years of his working career as a newspaper reporter, editor and college journalism instructor. The next 24 years were spent as an insurance regulator, a health insurance company lobbyist and as a researcher for a national property/casualty trade association. Reddick is co-editor of *The Magic of Indians' Baseball, 1887-1987* and the author of 15 fictional short stories. He and his wife, Rebecca, live in Camby, Indiana.

INDEX